FINDING WALLACE!

Some names and identifying details have been changed to protect the privacy of individuals.

Published by R Thomas Rankin

ISBN: 978-0-9991592-1-7

Cover design, illustration & interior formatting:
Mark Thomas / Coverness.com

FINDING WALLACE!

OR

HOW WE CAME
TO ADOPT
OUR SON FROM
RUSSIA
AND THE
MISADVENTURES
THAT
FOLLOWED

R. THOMAS RANKIN

To Elisabeth and Wallace

Why I Wrote This Book and Other Things

The Prologue Featuring Evil Spies, Marco Polo, and Someone's Boxer Shorts

The Rankin family had travelled en masse to Portland, Oregon, for a family gathering. We returned, tired, to our hotel after a long day of family time. Elisabeth and I needed to freshen up and wanted clean towels after a few days of using the same ones. I called the front desk, and they promised to send up some fresh ones.

Wallace, as usual, possessed enough energy to power a small city.

"Mom and Dad, can we go swimming or play enemy spies in the lobby?"

"I am quite certain that the hotel does not allow spies to chase each other in the lobby," opined Elisabeth.

"We have plans for tonight, but we can go swimming in the morning," I said as I was changing clothes.

"Oh man!" said Wallace, facing the prospect of not capturing the evil spy or even a chlorinated Marco Polo.

As it turns out, two people from the housekeeping staff decided to visit our room at the same time. The housekeepers arrived just as I had removed my trousers. There was a polite knock, and Wallace went toward the door.

"I got it, Dad," said Wallace in an innocent tone but with a look on his face that said mischief and mayhem.

"Wallace, wait, let me put on my pants!"

Elisabeth, in her own state of undress, escaped to the bathroom while Wallace opened the door.

So there I was, in my SpongeBob boxer shorts, having a conversation with the two housekeepers.

"Umm, Hi" was all I could muster as I tripped over words and turned red with embarrassment.

Wallace was on the floor convulsing in laughter and pointing at me.

"You asked for some towels, Mr. SquarePants?" giggled one of the housekeepers.

"Yes. Thank you." I tried to give Wallace the evil eye, but had trouble keeping a straight face. Wallace 1, Dad 0.

It was definitely a moment to remember.

Wallace is a mischievous, fun-loving young man who happened to be born in Kemerovo, Russia, a medium-sized city in the heart of Russia's coal mining region and very far away from our home in Jamestown, New York. This book is the story of our love for Wallace, and how we traveled halfway around the world to Kemerovo to adopt him and welcome our son into the warm, loving embrace of our family. This book is as much his story as it is ours. Later on, I'll share more stories about Wallace and our family, without further mention of my boxer shorts.

Now, for a More Traditional Introduction Lacking Any Mention of Spies

I wrote this book to show that children adopted from Russia can lead full, active, and rewarding lives with their parents in the United States. Our son, Wallace, has had his share of challenges in his young life, but he is generally a happy, good-natured boy.

My name is Tom Rankin. I am married to a wonderful woman named Elisabeth Rankin. Our son is Wallace, and this is our story so far.

Adopting Wallace has been one of the most life-changing things Elisabeth and I have ever done. Wallace was born in Kemerovo, Siberia, and lived in an orphanage when we first met him. Elisabeth and I had struggled for years to conceive a child the "regular way" but could not. We finally came to the realization that we wanted to be parents, not necessarily pregnant. That is when we began the process to adopt a child.

We chose to adopt from Russia because we thought it

would be too difficult to adopt a baby here in Western New York. Our understanding of domestic adoptions was that we would potentially wait a long time to adopt an infant. Elisabeth and I also believed that adopting from Russia would bring more certainty and finality to our family. We may have been wrong about a domestic adoption (or not), but do not at all regret going to Russia to adopt our son.

Wallace is bright, articulate, and loves life. Bringing Wallace home was a pivotal point in all of our lives. The memory of the snowy ride from the airport in December will stay with me forever. Elisabeth feels the same way. However, our story does not end with coming home; that was only the beginning of many new and thrilling adventures for the Rankin family.

Wallace also has several mental health diagnoses that challenge him, and all of us. A large part of this book tries to show what it is like to live with a special needs child. Wallace's short life has profoundly affected our entire family.

Before I get to all of that, I'll begin with how Elisabeth and I came to adopt Wallace, which was quite the adventure.

Childless in Boston

Making Peace with a Situation We Could Not Change

"It didn't work again!" Elisabeth was crying, and I felt lost and hopeless.

"Are you sure? What did the clinic say?" Common sense had eluded me at the moment.

"I don't need the clinic to tell me that I'm not pregnant."

We were both at our respective work places, and I really wanted to be with and hold Elisabeth.

"Elisabeth, I refuse to give up. We must keep trying." Elisabeth and I had been seeking help in conceiving a baby for almost a year.

Later that night, at home, Elisabeth agreed, "I thought it over this afternoon. I want to keep trying, too."

We kept trying to get pregnant with the help of our fertility clinic. This part of the story does not pertain directly to our adoption adventure but hopefully shows how we came to the decision to try adoption. The next few pages involve some information that is both terribly personal and also more than you may want to know

5

about infertility treatments. However, our struggles with infertility proved pivotal for our story of adoption.

The pain of infertility wounds people emotionally. Wounds, however, heal over time. Elisabeth and I never let emotional pain stop us from continuing in our quest to become parents. Elisabeth and I did not feel complete as a family of two.

Two Different Green Line Trolleys Have Stops in the Longwood Medical Area

Elisabeth and I lived in suburban Boston just after we were married in 1998. I am happy to report that we are still married today. We tried to conceive a child almost as soon as we were married. As I said before, the *regular way* did not work for us, though not for lack of trying.

Elisabeth's employer offered great health insurance at the time, and we were able to try conceiving with the assistance of a fertility clinic at one of the best hospitals in Boston. We were game to try anything. We spent many hours at the Longwood medical area enlisting the aid of modern medical science to conceive a child. For many people, fertility treatments can be just the boost to aid in conceiving a child, and we hoped that would be the case for us, too.

We tried the self-injected (prescribed by a doctor)

treatments at home. This led to some interesting conversations because the injections had to go into someone's, ummm, posterior.

"Are you ready?"

"Yes, I've loaded the syringe. Are *you* ready for this?"

"As ready as I ever will be. Do you know where to aim?"

"The nurse gave me a very detailed guide on aiming and injecting. I don't think anyone has ever given me such a detailed description of my wife's bum."

"OK, already! Just do it."

"Alright, on three: one, two, three!"

In went the needle, and down went the plunger. What followed next was a lot of hope and prayers. The injections were designed to induce the production of eggs in Elisabeth.

We had regular clinic appointments that followed the injections. Actually, my appointments were separate from Elisabeth's appointments. (This is a delicate way of trying to explain the man's and woman's different roles in fertility treatments.) The clinic staff at my appointments always showed the most professional and caring demeanor. That never really lessened my mortified feeling. I had to somehow get my contribution to the process into a test tube.

The idea was to clinically insert my sperm at the most likely moment conception would occur. This is probably more information than you wanted to know. However, the science of fertility treatments sent us on an emotional ride that surpassed any roller coaster. Most conversations went like this:

I would go to the fertility clinic at the really large hospital and then call Elisabeth. She would ask, "How did it go?"

"Fine. I gave my sample to the nurse," I would reply.

"OK, my appointment is for later this afternoon."

At dinner that night, I would ask, "How did your part go?"

"It went well. Talk about an invasive procedure."

"Well, let's hope and pray."

"I am doing both!" Elisabeth would respond. The excitement *and* tension were palpable.

Some days later, Elisabeth would give me the bad news. Each cycle ended in devastation. We wanted badly to have children and felt blocked at every move by science, God, age, and all the other factors in conceiving a child. We must have tried this process about ten times. It never worked. Not once. We would be excited every time we started a new treatment cycle only to have our hopes crash on jagged rocks.

Elisabeth and I eventually received approval for in vitro fertilization (IVF). The IVF procedure was much more detailed than the simple insertion method. IVF also involves the harvesting of the woman's eggs. The woman's eggs and the man's sperm come together in a petri dish. A doctor then inserts the fertilized eggs into the woman.

Due to the expense, and our ages, our insurance company approved us for only one IVF treatment. We were excited and really hoped for a good outcome.

"Maybe IVF will be the procedure that works," I said. I really believed that statement.

"I really want this to work," said Elisabeth.

For the IVF procedure, our fertility clinic in Boston referred us to a different clinic in the suburbs. The IVF clinic was located in one of those monolithic office parks on Route 128, the highway that divides Greater Boston from many of its suburbs. More than ten years later, I still do not remember giving my sample, but I must have. Elisabeth went through another cycle of inducing multiple egg production and then went to the IVF clinic for removal. Then came the big day—insertion.

I remember that our appointment was for a Saturday morning.

Elisabeth and I got up bright and early. I asked, "Do we have everything?"

Elisabeth calmly replied, "Umm, honey, we do not need to bring anything. The clinic already has the necessary *stuff*."

"Good point. Let's go!"

"Honey, it's only 6:30 a.m. The clinic isn't open yet, and our appointment is for 9:00 a.m."

I guess that I was excited, too.

We arrived at the IVF clinic with plenty of time to spare. Then came the last news we wanted to hear that morning. We really wanted the doctor to say that everything looked good for the IVF procedure. Instead, the doctor said that Elisabeth had a polyp in her uterus. This polyp could prevent an embryo from properly attaching to the uterus. We had to decide right then if we wanted to proceed. If we chose not to proceed, and have the polyp removed, it appeared that our insurance company would not approve us for another IVF procedure. We, Elisabeth mostly, elected to continue, but we were not happy.

The procedure itself went smoothly, if uncomfortably for Elisabeth. The staff let me sit with Elisabeth during the procedure. The doctor then inserted the "stuff" into Elisabeth using a thin metal tube-like 'thing' (please excuse the technical medical jargon).

The doctor then said, and I quote, "How does that feel?"

Elisabeth, from a most compromised position, replied, "How do you think this feels! It feels like I have a metal tube inside me!"

The doctor, realizing his faux pas, said, "Yes, I guess that was a stupid question. What I meant was, are you in any pain?"

"No, but please hurry."

The chagrined doctor quickly finished the procedure. Elisabeth and I jumped up (gingerly for Elisabeth) and headed home full of high hopes.

IVF failed for us, and we were miserable. The pain of the conversation when we learned that IVF failed is too difficult even now to recount. Accepting infertility caused Elisabeth and me to really grieve for a while. We needed to mourn the child(ren) that we could not have. Tears flowed from both of us. Elisabeth and I clung to each other as we spent years coming to terms with a fact in our lives that we could not change.

Other than continuing with the *regular way*, we put family planning on hold in 2003. I graduated from law school in 2003 and spend a nerve-racking summer studying for the bar exam.

Elisabeth and I had made the decision to move to Jamestown, New York, where Elisabeth had grown up. Jamestown lies between Buffalo and Erie, Pennsylvania. It is the largest city in Chautauqua County, which lies on the shores of Lake Erie. Every summer, half of Cleveland moves up to Chautauqua County to enjoy living on Chautauqua Lake. Jamestown is also known for its large number of trees, great tasting tap water (really), and brick streets.

I joined a local law firm, and Elisabeth found a job in her

field of higher education administration. After much talk and prayer, Elisabeth and I decided to pursue adoption.

Elisabeth Has Been Fingerprinted More Times Than the Average Criminal

The above section detailed a part of our journey through a subdivision of Hades. Now our story takes a turn for the better. I cannot say that Elisabeth and I walked through a wardrobe into a magical land of lions and lush green hills, but life did improve.

The turnaround really took hold when we bought our first (and only) house in 2004. We bought a house built in 1912 with all of the modern amenities of the early twentieth century (I embellish only a little...). The doorbells are actual bells attached to the original doors. Back before electricity was common in American homes, visitors would turn the knob of the doorbell to manually ring the bell. Wallace likes to ring these bells now because it gets the dog all excited.

When we first visited the house, the owner at the time had a young boy who had a very cute bedroom. The room had glow-in-the-dark stars on the ceiling, fun kids furniture, and adorable wallpaper.

"Can't you just imagine our own child in this room?" I asked.

"Yes. Yes, I can," said Elisabeth.

"We'll have a lot of work to do on this house."

"We're ready to work, and we need to have a home if we want to adopt."

Elisabeth and I went on to buy this house and still live in it today. On the day we closed, about four inches of snow fell. I celebrated home ownership by shoveling the sidewalk. The conversation about the child's room did help Elisabeth and me to sharpen our goals. First, we needed to move out of Elisabeth's mother's house and get our own home. Second, we needed to actually start the adoption process.

We did not know how to research and select an adoption agency. Yahoo and Google helped give us leads, but the many phone calls and emails fell to us to make. There are hundreds of adoption agencies in the United States. Elisabeth and I had agreed that adopting from Russia would be a good choice for us. First and foremost, Russia still used orphanages to care for kids who could not live with their parents. Adoption by foster parents just did not happen in Russia. Elisabeth and I thought we could help one child leave an orphanage and come to a *forever home*. We pared down our list of potential adoption agencies until we finally contracted with an agency in Orlando, Florida.

Our adoption process ultimately proved successful.

What Elisabeth and I know now however, makes us shudder at how easily everything could have failed. Elisabeth and I had the noblest of intentions in 2004, and we still do. (This whole book is about our adopted son.) The road to adopting from Russia in 2004-05 definitely took us through the *shady side of town*. The best example I can give is that our adoption agency in Orlando closed under dubious circumstances not long after we completed our adoption.

Before I digress too much, I turn to the part where Elisabeth and I had to put together a dossier on our lives.

"We'll do the hard part. You just have to track down the documents, and we'll put together your dossier," promised Allan (...not his real name, but - because our adoption agency failed under uncertain circumstances - I do not want to give "Allan" any actual publicity) the head of our adoption agency. With that promise, Elisabeth and I signed the contract with our adoption agency. Welcome to September 2004.

"We have put together so many dossiers for prospective adoptive parents that we can do your dossier faster than you can" was another of Allan's statements of fact. By *fact*, I refer to satirist Stephen Colbert's great word, "truthiness." Allan sounded great, but he actually ignored logic and intellectual examination of the issue. For example, Elisabeth and I had to procure all of the documents on the list below. The documents then had to be apostiled (an apostille being a state certification attached to notarized documents and this being the first of several cameo such appearances in this book) in New York, but we first had to send the documents to our adoption agency in Orlando. This actually added time to the process.

In fairness to our adoption agency, their work did reduce our stress in the beginning. It is daunting to put together an adoption dossier for use in a foreign country. Allan's promises, though, turned out to be rosier than real life.

Any adoption, foreign or domestic, consists of two basic parts. The first part is where the prospective adoptive parents show that they have the ability to parent a child. Elisabeth and I had to put together our dossier of the following information:

- Short life histories for each of us (Elisabeth made me take out the part where I won a Nobel Prize.)
- Medical exams and medical histories
- Income verification
- Criminal background checks, including fingerprints taken with the New York State Police and a letter from our county sheriff
- Child abuse background checks
- Proof of home ownership, or formal lease, including proof that our property taxes were paid

- Confirmation that we had no previous contract with Rumpelstiltskin
- Personal references
- Home study by a licensed social worker

Every single document had to be notarized and then apostiled. The paralegal at my law firm graciously agreed to accompany me to my doctor in order to notarize my physical examination. That led to an interesting conversation:

"Michelle, can you notarize a document for me? It is a simple little thing."

"Sure, Tom. What is it, a will or deed?" said Michelle.

"Actually, I need you to go with me to my doctor's office and notarize my physical. It's part of our adoption dossier."

"Whoa. I am happy to help with your adoption, but I draw the line at watching you get a physical. Where and what would I imprint with my notary stamp?" said Michelle.

Thoughts of a sexual harassment lawsuit and divorce filled my head.

"Oh, sorry," I replied. "I didn't mean...I was just... ummmm. The physical already took place. I need you to notarize the form that the doctor has to sign."

"Well, that's different. Of course I will notarize your doctor's signature."

As we finished gathering all of the required documents,

our adoption agency scheduled our home study with a social worker.

The home study was an interesting afternoon for us. Our adoption agency arranged for a very nice person to visit us and insisted that no other social worker would do. Allan at the adoption agency seemed convinced that neither Elisabeth nor I had the skills required to hire a social worker here in metropolitan Jamestown.

This social worker our adoption agency hired lived in the New York City area, about a six-hour drive from Jamestown. In order to get to scenic Jamestown, Linda - not her real name, but used here as I totally I forget Linda's real name - the social worker decided to take a train to LaGuardia (airport), flew to Buffalo, and then rented a car to drive to Jamestown. This was probably the most convoluted travel schedule for a social worker who lived in the same state as us. Our adoption agency said that it would simplify the adoption process but clearly did not think through the social worker part of the process. (For our post-adoption reports, Elisabeth and I found a social worker that lived about twenty minutes from our house.)

Anyway, Elisabeth and I duly cleaned our house and told our dog, Chip, to be on his best behavior. Chip seemed a little put off by the whole affair.

"Welcome to our home," said Elisabeth as Linda arrived.

"Thank you. You live so far away!" replied Linda.

"Well, not to us," I said. Elisabeth gave me the evil eye.

Linda seemed confused. "I thought Jamestown was in Pennsylvania."

"I think you are confusing us with Johnstown, which is in Pennsylvania."

"Oh. I see. So you didn't have the flood?"

"Ummm, no. Jamestown is famous for being the home of Lucille Ball."

"I just love Lucy!"

I offered to show to Linda Ms. Ball's grave in the cemetery about two blocks away, and then Elisabeth kicked me under the table.

We then all sat around our kitchen table and talked about life for a while. Early October brings out vibrant colors in western New York. The conversation about autumn, kids' activities, and football seemed casual, but Elisabeth and I knew that this meeting was an important milestone in our quest to adopt a child. The social worker's report was a key element in our dossier, one that was very subjective.

Elisabeth and I enjoyed talking with Linda. She took notes as we talked. Some of the questions seemed obvious:

"Why are you adopting?"

"Tell me about your experience with fertility treatments."

"Where will your child go to school?"

"How do you feel about corporal punishment?"

"Have you talked with pediatricians in the area?"

"How will you handle discussing your child's birth parents with your child?"

Elisabeth and I answered honestly. We had discussed many of these issues prior to meeting Linda. Still, we were nervous. Linda then veered off into the world of professional football. Linda wanted to know if we were fans of the Buffalo Bills.

"So, do you root for the Bills?"

"I do," said Elisabeth with a big smile.

"I actually root for the New England Patriots. We are what you call a mixed marriage."

Linda, the Jets fan, did not know what to think of us: two misguided football fans living in relative harmony. The visit had gone well, and then Linda asked for a tour of our house. When we showed her the child's room, Elisabeth and I were sort of embarrassed. The room was completely empty, but we did not want Linda to think that we were shirking our duties as prospective parents.

"We don't want to buy things or decorate until we know our child is coming home," said Elisabeth.

I chimed in, "The pain of infertility combined with the uncertainty in the adoption process makes us not want to get our hopes up. Neither one of us can bear to look in a fully furnished child's room for months or years when we do not yet have a child."

We held our breath for a moment.

"I agree with you entirely. Don't furnish the room until about one or two weeks before your child comes home. Otherwise the emotional pain can be tremendous."

Elisabeth and I breathed a huge sigh of relief. We then showed Linda the rest of the house, including our finished attic. The only negative comment Linda made about our house was that we needed a handrail on both sides of the stairs leading to the attic. With that sage advice Linda deemed Elisabeth and me fit enough to adopt a child. Linda's written report became part of our dossier. I think we received the report on Christmas Eve that year. Thank you FedEx.

Because we planned to adopt from a foreign country, Elisabeth and I also had to apply for permission to adopt with the Department of Homeland Security. This meant, among other things, a trip to Buffalo to be fingerprinted again. Elisabeth and I drove up to Buffalo on the day before Thanksgiving in 2004. Of course it snowed the entire time we were driving. We did not know it then, but exactly one year and one day later, we would pick up Wallace from a Russian orphanage. On this snowy day in 2004, however, our biggest concern was getting out of Buffalo before the afternoon traffic started.

The specific entity in the Department of Homeland Security, United States Immigration and Citizenship

Services (USICS), processed our application to be approved as adoptive parents. USICS, just like the Russian government, wanted to make sure that Elisabeth and I had the wherewithal to adopt and care for a child. More importantly, we had to show to USICS that we were adopting a true orphan. As annoying as governmental agencies can be, Elisabeth and I understand that our federal government tries to prevent human trafficking.

It took us about six months to get everything together, notarized, and apostiled (which meant about a month of mailing documents to a state office in Albany). Our adoption agency promised to get the documents apostiled—and they did for the first round. Elisabeth and I later learned that adoption dossiers are like cartons of milk: They all eventually expire. This expiration date issue became known to us about a year later. First, Elisabeth and I had to finish everything in 2004.

Elisabeth's first set of fingerprints at Homeland Security were not legible. That meant another trip to Buffalo for Elisabeth. The second set of fingerprints were legible, and Homeland Security soon cleared us to adopt from a foreign country. Our adoption agency informed us in the spring of 2005 that our dossier was complete and accepted by the Russian government.

The Urban Dictionary Defines Sketchy as "Someone or Something That Just Is Not Right."[01]

Next came part two of the process: We waited for the Russian government to send us referrals. Elisabeth and I later found out that the Russian government, in 2005, did not want prospective adoptive parents to receive *any* information about the child they may adopt other than the child's gender, age, and location. The local orphanages and adoption agencies, however, had put together a "back channel" to give prospective adoptive parents a picture and some relevant information about their prospective son or daughter.

This part of adopting from Russia, or any other country, highlights the underbelly of international adoptions. Everyone we met at Wallace's orphanage was sincerely interested in helping these young children. Part of helping, though, meant dealing with people who worked outside of normal government procedures. To this day, Elisabeth and I feel a little uneasy about how our adoption of Wallace involved using information obtained outside of official channels. On the other hand, we could not have possibly considered adopting a child (from anywhere) without

---

01 http://www.urbandictionary.com/define.php?term=Sketchy, last visited on February 25, 2017.

knowing some basic information about the child.

I remember a conversation I had with the director of our adoption agency. This was not "Allan" the chief executive officer, but "Herb," the day-to-day director (I refuse to use the real names of the agency staff).

"Does the Russian government send you these pictures and information about children available for adoption?" I asked. I quickly learned how naïve this question was.

"Well, no, not exactly," said Herb, "The orphanages are state owned, but they utilize a private company to send the pictures and other information to adoption agencies outside Russia."

"Are we adopting children from a Russian black market?"

"No. The orphanages are truly state owned. You'll go through official Russian government agencies and courts for the actual adoption. The Russian government, however, does not want foreigners to have any information about the children available for adoption until the prospective parents arrive in Russia for their first visit."

"Elisabeth and I would not feel too comfortable flying to Russia with no information about the child or children we could adopt."

"Exactly," said Herb. "We use the services of a company out of Atlanta that has the contacts in Russia. The orphanages send the information to this Atlanta company, who then sends it to us."

The orphanages would send a picture and some basic information to this Atlanta company. If the Russian government was aware of this practice, then it ignored this flow of information so long as all the parties involved did not flaunt the practice. I will discuss this Atlanta company more, later...

The referral process took us through most of the summer of 2005. We received a few referrals where the children in question clearly had significant medical problems. Elisabeth and I hated to refuse any referral, but we knew that we were not in a position to adopt a child with serious medical issues. We were not looking for perfection at all, but we knew our limitations as working parents.

The referrals came from our adoption agency via email. We typically received a photograph and short medical history of the child. We also found out what part of Russia the child lived. The United States government and World Health Organization both keep statistical data on infant height, weight, and head circumference.[02] Just knowing where the child measured on the growth charts gave us an idea of potential medical issues.[03]

Late in the summer of 2005, we received a referral that seemed to be a good match for us and the child.

---

02 http://www.cdc.gov/growthcharts/who_charts.htm, last visited on February 25, 2017.

03 http://www.livestrong.com/article/504393-infant-head-circumference-low-growth/, last visited on February 25, 2017.

Meeting Kiril—Our First Trip to Russia

"Should I wear my blue button-down shirt or white-button down shirt for our first meeting at the orphanage?" I inquired to Elisabeth.

"First of all, there is more to life than button-down shirts. Secondly, I don't think a twelve-month-old baby will care too much about your clothes," answered Elisabeth.

In 2005, Russia required foreign adoptive parents to make two trips to Russia. The first trip was to meet our prospective child. The second trip was to formally adopt the child. In between was a frantic paperwork chase and nervous waiting.

Our Floridian adoption agency had presented our adoption profile to so-called authorities in Russia, and we finally had a referral. However, we had actually never met anyone in person at our adoption agency. We conversed by telephone and email. We used regular mail to send documents and checks for sums of money. Elisabeth and I received Wallace's information by email from our adoption agency and worked with them on our dossier. One of the many reasons we feel lucky is that our adoption agency helped us complete our adoption of Wallace before suddenly going out of business. We never heard from our adoption agency again after we brought Wallace home in early December 2005.

I start this part of the story at a time when our adoption agency was not only still in business, but also putting together our trips to Russia. After years of sadness due to infertility, Elisabeth and I finally were able to have a child. Wallace was able to leave an orphanage in Siberia to join our family and start a new life in Western New York. Just how that happened was an adventure of a lifetime.[04]

Kemerovo Administrators Announced That They Had "Indisputable Proof" That Mountains in the Region Were Inhabited by Yeti[05]

Elisabeth and I learned through our adoption agency that our prospective son lived in an orphanage in Kemerovo, Siberia, Russia.

"Where is Kemerovo?" Elisabeth asked me after we had

---

04 This chapter started out as my notes that I subsequently put on a private web page. I have revised my notes into actual sentences and paragraphs. At least that is what my editor recommended. Hopefully this chapter appears cohesive and organized.

05 https://www.bellenews.com/2011/10/11/world/europe-news/ russia-proofs-of-yetis-existence-in-kemerovo-region/, last visited on February 25, 2017.

received a referral for a child living there. I had done some research.

"Fire up Google Maps (at least I *think* it was Google maps; I definitely used an online mapping service...) and then locate the point where Mongolia and Kazakhstan meet. Then head due north about an inch and a half," I replied. While my reference points were clearly accurate, they were not used by most of the travelling public. Elisabeth and I eventually figured out where Kemerovo was in relation to Jamestown.

In 2005, about five hundred thousand people lived in the city of Kemerovo, which is the capitol city of the Kemerovo Oblast region. For the really adventurous, you can take the Trans-Siberian Railway to Kemerovo. I have read that Kemerovo is a sister city with Billings, Montana. Billings, however, has no indisputable proof of Yeti living in the surrounding area.

We received Wallace's information in the summer of 2005 through an established back channel used by our adoption agency. Before Wallace became our son, Elisabeth and I learned that there was a very young boy named Kiril living in an orphanage in Kemerovo. We knew that Kiril was born at home about thirty days premature, via breach birth, and immediately transported to the hospital. From the hospital, Kiril went to the orphanage. The black and white picture of Kiril (shoulders up) showed no obvious physical issues. The referral had no medical information other than it was suspected that his birth mother used drugs while pregnant. Kiril was not yet a year old when we received his information.

Elisabeth and I had discussed this referral and prayed. While we knew we could decline the referral once we met the child, Elisabeth and I also knew that would be a terribly difficult choice to make. We were going to confirm our decision, and did not want to decline the referral unless in an exceptional circumstance. First, we had to fly halfway around the world to meet this young boy.

We Flew 4,726 Miles to Eat Georgian Food

Many of my comments in the next two chapters relate to cultural differences between the United States and Russia. The vast majority of Russian people we met were decent, kind people. Irina, Sergei, Bob, and Viktor were incredibly helpful and supportive of our mission to adopt our son who became Wallace. Elisabeth and I fondly remember working with these folks, and others, during our not quite calm adventures in Russia.

September 7, 2005

We left Jamestown at about 3:30 in the afternoon to go to the big city of Buffalo for our first flight. Elisabeth's brother-in-law, Andy, drove us to the airport. We were concerned about our ability to drive home on the return after being up for about thirty hours, so we arranged for rides. It was a warm, sunny day, and we got to the airport with plenty of time to spare for our 7:23 p.m. flight. We actually added a couple of extra days to this trip so we could tour Moscow before getting down to business in Kemerovo.

Our flight from Moscow to Kemerovo was scheduled on Aeroflot, an airline that had a very strict weight requirement for checked baggage, only forty-four pounds (an even twenty kilograms in the rest of the world) per bag, and we could have only one checked bag each. Though it was warm in Jamestown and Moscow, the weather had turned cool in Kemerovo. We needed to bring both warm weather and cool weather clothes, thereby adding weight and bulk to our baggage. I carefully weighed each suitcase before leaving for Buffalo. Sadly, the emergency cans of Spam had to come out, but then both bags weighed less than forty-four pounds each.

"Did you really put a can of Spam in your suitcase?" asked Elisabeth

"Of course," I answered. "What if there is a blackout while we are in Kemerovo and we can't leave our hotel for a few days?"

"For a smart, caring, loveable guy, you can be a real dork sometimes."

United Flight 7797 left on time and landed at Dulles on time. The flight used one of those small jets, an ER 145, which made for very cozy seating. Compared to our Aeroflot flight a few days later, this flight was spacious and at least had functional air conditioning.

We landed at Dulles and had to walk only a short distance to the gate for our flight to Frankfurt, Germany.

"Great!" I said. "We don't have to change terminals, just walk to the other end of the concourse." This was the first of many naïve statements I would make on our two trips to Russia. Well, about a half mile and forty some odd gates later, we arrived. It felt like a low-budget cartoon where the characters keep walking but the background does not change. Hong Kong Phooey comes to mind.

Arriving with twenty minutes to spare before boarding, we made our last mobile phone calls. Our mobile phones did not work in Europe. Remember, our first trip took place in the dark ages when there was no such thing as Wi-Fi, Twitter, Facebook, or any number of ways to stay connected online. We then boarded United Flight 932, a Boeing 777, bound for Frankfurt.

Luckily, United let us sit in "economy plus," where the economy seats had a little more leg room than "economy minus." What can I tell you about an eight-hour flight? Drinks, dinner, reading, movie, annoy wife, reading, fitful sleep, snack, landing. United charged $5 for adult beverages in economy on international flights. In days past, the hooch was complimentary.

"The white wine resembles turpentine—but a good year for turpentine," opined Elisabeth.

I then commented, "The ginger ale is of a particularly good vintage from an arid region of Canada." Little did we realize this would be our last chance to crack wise about something as innocuous as the in-flight beverage service. Later on, as we put our fate in the hands of Aeroflot, we'd find ourselves thankful that the jets flew at all.

September 8, 2005

The Frankfurt airport is big, very big, when you have not slept all night and have to find your flight to Moscow. At one point, we almost went through German passport control and into southwestern Germany, but the slightly amused immigration officer made us turn around. We persevered and determined the location of our next gate. We had about thirty minutes to kill and went to the airport restaurant. The equivalent of $11 bought us a warm Diet Coke, warm mineral water, and a cold, stale donut. We felt so sophisticated.

Lufthansa took us to Moscow on an A300 aircraft

and really provided good service. The flight was only three hours long, but Lufthansa gave us a hot meal and complimentary adult beverages. I chose a cold soft drink, and the flight attendant splurged and put ice in the cup. I felt like I had been upgraded to *Decadent Class*. The cabin crew did a great job.

We landed at Terminal 2 of Sheremetyevo Airport near Moscow. The Soviet government built Terminal 2 for the 1980 Olympics and had yet to remodel this showcase of communist design. Clearly, the Soviet government had used unemployed prison architects to design Sheremetyevo.

I had previously arranged for the *Fast Track* service for Russian passport control and customs. Two very attractive Russian women met us at the airport and took us to the diplomats' line to have our passports duly stamped. This avoided the very crowded regular passport line. After retrieving our bags, another very attractive Russian woman took us through customs (nothing to declare), and no one stopped us. Elisabeth was both happy and annoyed with me: Happy because we quickly cleared passport control and customs; annoyed because I was clearly pleased with our guides.

After customs, our interpreter, Sergei, met us. At this point, it was about 6:45 p.m. Moscow time, or about 10:45 a.m. in Jamestown the day after our departure. In other words, we had been awake for about thirty hours and were starting to get a little goofy.

All of the hotels we contacted in Moscow wanted from about $200 to $400 per night. That was too rich for us. Neither Elisabeth nor I felt comfortable having other people make hotel reservations for us due to some bad experiences when we had lived overseas. After some online research, we decided to rent an apartment for our two-day stay in Moscow for less money than most hotels. Sergei and our driver, Viktor, drove us into Moscow— about a thirty-minute drive. Our apartment was right on Arbat Street in Moscow, a big tourist area.

"You rented an apartment on Arbat Street?!?" exclaimed Sergei, "Do you know where Arbat Street is?"

"Ummm, no. We've never been to Moscow before."

"Arbat Street is closed to motor vehicles! I hope Viktor can find a parking spot."

It took Viktor some time to find the best place to park near our apartment. I learned some new Russian swear words that night.

One of the requirements we had for our apartment building is that it have elevator service. Our particular apartment was on the sixth floor. Technically, our apartment had a working elevator. The elevator's bottom floor, however, was on the second floor. This meant we had to haul our bags up a flight of stairs to get to the elevator. (Always read the fine print even if it is in a language you do not understand!) Sergei was annoyed but tried to be upbeat.

"You know this could be a nice place, but next time can you coordinate with me on this 'apartment rental' business?"

"We are sorry for the trouble. The online brochure implied that driving to this apartment was not difficult and that Sheremetyevo is a wonderful airport. Thank you for getting us here."

Sergei helped us get situated in our apartment and then took me to exchange some money. Sergei also pointed out the supermarket nearby. We then bid Sergei good night and went shopping. We bought bread, cheese, ham, bananas, bottled water, and juice. Not exactly a gourmet dinner, but we liked it. The best part: Our apartment came with satellite TV, and we watched *MythBusters* in English while we dined. We then showered and crashed.

September 9, 2005

I said "crashed," and we did sleep for a little while. We also had a good case of jet lag and woke up about 4 a.m. I stayed in bed until about 6 a.m. and then got up to read for a while. After a shower, I set off to conquer the local McDonald's for Elisabeth's coffee. There is something to be said for consistency of product and American fast food in the former Soviet Union. I figured out to ask for "Coffee

Americano" and voilà, Elisabeth had her morning dose of caffeine.

The washing machine in the apartment apparently did not work. Ever the trooper, Elisabeth washed our travel clothes by hand, and I found a drying rack that fit on our small terrace.

We met Sergei at 9:00 a.m. and walked down Arbat Street and then over to the Kremlin. It was mild but muggy that day. There was a line of folks waiting to get into the Kremlin when we arrived. The line eventually brought us to the security checkpoint, just like an airport security check but without an X-ray machine or fun pat down.

The Kremlin is the official seat of government in Russia and was once just a big fort. Before the Bolshevik Revolution, the Kremlin was also the headquarters of the Russian Orthodox Church. Consequently, there are many government buildings and churches within the Kremlin compound. I cannot be the first person to note that the seat of government in the old Soviet Union was (and is now again) the headquarters of the largest religious body in the country. It seems the Russians don't share our views of the separation of church and state. In the heart of Russian power, these two institutions live and function side by side.

We toured the various churches in the Kremlin. We also saw some of Napoleon's cannons he left behind as he retreated from Russia and also one gigantic bell. I kept asking where Pierre Bezukhov - a major character in *War and Peace* - was, but no one got the joke.[06] Apparently, Russians take their Tolstoy very seriously. It is cool, however, to say, "I visited the Kremlin," but it is not exactly an action-packed experience.

From the Kremlin, we walked over to Red Square. Here, one can see Lenin's Mausoleum and Saint Basil's Cathedral. Lenin's Mausoleum was closed when we were there, but we were not bitterly disappointed. One little fact we did learn: In the Soviet Days, on May Day, leaders would watch the parades from atop Lenin's Mausoleum. That would be similar to United States leaders watching an Independence Day parade from the top of George Washington's crypt.

Saint Basil's is the iconic symbol most people picture when thinking of Moscow. You know, the onion dome church. One long side of Red Square is a wall of the Kremlin, and the other long side is the GUM department store (now a mall), which used to be one of the few places in Moscow to buy Western-made goods. It is a very, very large building.

I next wanted to see Tolstoy's house, and Elisabeth

06 I read *War and Peace* in the 1990s when I lived in Japan. English language paperback books cost a small fortune in Japan, so I bought the longest book I could find.

rolled her eyes. Sergei flagged down a person driving a government car. For about $3.33, this person took us over to that part of town. We would not have flagged down a random car without Sergei's help. That seemed just a little strange to us.

Elisabeth asked, "You mean government workers use their official vehicles as personal taxi cabs?"

"Sort of," said Sergei. "They can give rides for pay for short trips that do not take a long time. This is normal for us."

"You're sure this is safe?" I inquired.

"Yeah, mostly." This response did not exactly fill us with confidence.

We arrived safely at Tolstoy's house to a pleasant surprise: free admission because it was Tolstoy's birthday. (Yay, us!) It was interesting to see a nineteenth-century residence and where Tolstoy actually wrote some of his works. I took a picture of Tolstoy's bed. I kept asking where Pierre Bezukhov was, but again, no one got the joke.

We ate lunch in a bowling alley. It was an upscale bowling alley at least. By this time, it was near 3:00 p.m. Sergei had called Viktor, who picked us up and took us to run some errands. We bought post card stamps for 17 rubles each, exchanged money at a better rate than the night before, and bought film (nothing but the finest of twentieth-century technology for us). For some literal sightseeing, we went to Moscow State University, which overlooks the city. We took some pictures and admired the communist architectural "achievements." Viktor and Sergei then took us back to our apartment on Arbat Street.

For dinner that night, we went to a Georgian restaurant—Georgia the country, not the US state. For appetizers, we ate some Georgian cheese w/mint, Georgian vegetables, something unidentifiable, and Georgian cheesy bread. Elisabeth had a veal dish for dinner, and I had Georgian chicken goulash. Elisabeth like the Georgian white wine, and I liked the *German* beer. For dessert, we ate a piece of Georgian cake. It was just like eating in Tbilisi but without the armed invasion.[07]

We watched some more *MythBusters* back at our apartment. Elisabeth did some more laundry and then we crashed.

September 10, 2005

I said "crashed," and we did sleep for a little while. We also had a good case of jet lag and woke up about 4 a.m. (Does this sound familiar?) I got up before dawn and read some more. At about 7:00 a.m., Elisabeth got up, and we put the still-wet clothes outside to dry. We had to check out at

07 "2008 Georgia Russia Conflict Fast Facts," http://www.cnn.com/2014/03/13/world/europe/2008-georgia-russia-conflict/, last visited on February 25, 2017.

noon, and the last pieces were pronounced "dry" at 11:45 a.m.

Sergei and Viktor met us at noon for our last day before flying out to Kemerovo. We put our bags in Viktor's car, and he took us to the Russian Armed Forces museum. Viktor left us then to go take a university exam. Sergei took us around the large museum. We saw the development of the Russian military from czarist times to the present. There was even a section devoted to the forces who *opposed* the Bolshevik Revolution. Sergei dryly observed that such displays were not in the museum during the Soviet era.

I enjoyed the room dedicated to the siege of Stalingrad in World War II. Sergei enjoyed the display of actual tanks in the courtyard. Elisabeth enjoyed leaving.

Sergei then took us to a Russian-Ukrainian restaurant for a late lunch. Elisabeth really like the herring pie; I am not such a devotee of herring. I tried the traditional borscht, and Elisabeth tried the green borsch soup. Traditional borscht is made from beets, but also has onions, cabbage, pork, and other stuff in it. On the table, one then adds sour cream. Very tasty. For the main course, I ate some Russian dumplings, cabbage, and pork. Elisabeth tried some chicken dish. We were all quite happy with our meals.

We said goodbye to Sergei at this point. We leave Sergei with a joke he told us: Lenin, Stalin, Brezhnev, and Yeltsin were on a train together. At a station stop, they saw some government construction workers taking an unauthorized break. Lenin said, "Send assassins to kill them!" Stalin said, "Put them in front of a firing squad!" Brezhnev said, "Send them to the gulags!" Yeltsin said, "I'll drink to that!"

Viktor then drove us to Sheremetyevo to catch our evening flight to Kemerovo. Our Lufthansa flight landed at the international terminal, but our Aeroflot flight to Kemerovo was out of the domestic portion, about three miles away. On the way, Viktor took us through several subdivisions where relatively wealthy people can buy houses instead of living in an apartment. Apparently, Sheremetyevo is the high-rent vacation district near Moscow.

We had several hours to kill. This set the stage for the Great Gin Rummy Tournament of 2005. Elisabeth surged to an early commanding lead. I slowly clawed my way back and took the lead on the final hand. Then we had to go check in for our flight. (The careful reader will note that the outcome of the game remains in doubt today.)

Check-in was really just semi-organized chaos. We pushed our way through security and waited in line for about thirty minutes before we got to actually check in. While waiting in line, we met a couple from Florida going to Kemerovo to adopt a teenage girl. This couple was on their second trip and would be bringing the girl home with them.

We learned that no-smoking signs are just a suggestion in the airport. Luckily, we soon got on the bus that took us to our plane, a Tupelov-154M. The TU-154M was the Russian equivalent of the old Boeing 727. The original TU-154M was designed in the mid-1960s Soviet Union. The TU-154M combined all the charm of a Soviet era design with 1980s technology. Unfortunately, we were traveling in 2005.

The NATO designation for the TU-154M is "Careless." Really. Google TU-154M and NATO, and see what you find.

In a stroke of luck, all of the foreigners on the flight were seated in the economy section located between first class and the galley. It was quiet, and not so crowded. The Aeroflot meal was actually quite palatable. I and Elisabeth both had the chicken and pasta. On the down side, the crew turned up the temperature to about 85 degrees Fahrenheit. We soon learned that some people on the flight did not fully understand the practical uses of deodorant (though, in fairness to the good people of Russia, I have been on many flights in the USA that have offended my olfactory senses). The flight was quite uncomfortable.

This particular flight really tested our resolve to adopt a child. We needed to travel literally halfway around the world just to get to the orphanage. The flights to and from Kemerovo had all the charm of an IRS audit conducted in

Russian. Kemerovo is actually a nice city but does not stand out as a major tourist destination. Parents do anything for their children, even the ones they have yet to meet.

The Immovable Bed Meets the Grumpy American

September 11, 2005

Our flight landed about 6:00 a.m. Kemerovo time, a four-hour time difference from Moscow. Our interpreter, Irina, met us at the airport along with a driver. We piled into our driver's minivan with a couple from Ireland whose interpreter was then missing. During the twenty minutes to downtown Kemerovo, Irina showed us some of the restaurants and grocery stores in the neighborhood of our hotel, but Elisabeth and I exuded grogginess.

We stayed at the Hotel Kuzbass in Kemerovo. Unfortunately, the only rooms available were the *non-refurbished* rooms. Our room was very small, with peeling wallpaper and peeling linoleum. (We did get to view a deluxe refurbished room and put in a request for this room type for the second trip.) It was just after 7:00 a.m. when we were finally alone in our room. We both said that we would lie down for a quick nap; we woke up at 2:00 p.m.

About the room: There were only twin beds available to us, and the beds were bolted to the walls. We had to sleep separately—communist family planning? There was only a bath with a handheld shower (no wall mount). We could not control the heat or air, except by opening the window. Romance was not an option in this room.

Each floor had a matron who controlled the keys and cleaned the rooms. If we needed anything, we would ask the floor matron, not the front desk. One wonders if this is a holdover from the communist days. A hotel employee always knew if we were in our room or not. Maybe, in the Soviet days, floor matrons would keep tabs on the guests in case the KGB ever wanted to investigate.

Well, it was cold and rainy on this Sunday, and we forgot to bring umbrellas with us. I went out in vain to find umbrellas, but all I found was that my coat was not waterproof. That was the major highlight of the afternoon.

In the evening, we met up with three other couples: one from Wisconsin, the Florida couple, and a different couple from Ireland. All of these folks were in Kemerovo to pick up children; the Irish couple were to adopt two toddler siblings. We ate at a Russian restaurant near the hotel. After dinner, we walked down to the Tom River (its actual name) at the Kemerovo WWII memorial.

Elisabeth and I, not surprisingly, were not immediately sleepy and slept quite poorly that night, though managed to create a double negative sentence. Jet lag really stinks, especially in a twin bed that is bolted to the floor across the room from your spouse.

September 12, 2005

The big day of the first trip—we got to see the child today.

"What exactly do you say to a twelve-month-old baby that does not talk yet and probably does not understand English?" wondered Elisabeth.

"I think we talk to the child like we normally would and forget about what language he may or may not understand," I said.

"This is all so surreal. We flew halfway around the world to meet a child that does not understand English, but we may yet adopt him." Well, when she put it that way, the whole situation did feel a bit unreal.

Elisabeth and I hugged and then went downstairs to the hotel lobby.

We met the other couple (from Minnesota) also traveling on their first trip today. Irina and our driver took us on the short trip to the orphanage. The Russian social worker rode with us as well and talked to us about adopting. The social worker only talked to the men, which seemed odd and gave the whole trip a bit of strange consistency.

The social worker was able to give us a little more information about Kiril. His birth mother indeed delivered Kiril in her apartment, and they both went to the hospital by ambulance. The birth mother, according to the social worker, needed to stay in the hospital after birth. The birth mother then left the hospital at the earliest possible opportunity. She did not take Kiril or visit him again. It was the hospital staff who named the baby, "Kiril", not any blood relative.

At the orphanage, each couple met separately with the orphanage director, orphanage doctor, and social worker. Elisabeth and I waited to let the other couple meet first with the orphanage staff and social worker.

"The big moment is almost here. How do you feel?" I asked as we sat in the director's outer office.

"Scared and excited. I, you, and we have no experience at all in adopting. I want to meet this boy, but I have so many emotions pushing through right now."

"I as well. Elisabeth, many different things can happen after today, but we need to meet this boy and see how we feel then."

"I know. What else can we do?"

Our turn came, and we went into the director's private office. The director had set up behind his desk a display of pictures of foreign families that had adopted children from this orphanage. The group of us spent some time talking about the child who we learned was named Kiril. At last the time came to meet little Kiril.

The staff brought us into the office of the orphanage speech therapist. I took Kiril from the staff, and then we all stood around awkwardly staring at each other. The social worker then went to visit the Minnesota couple, and the doctor helped us examine Kiril. Finally, the doctor left. Now we had to figure out what to do with a twelve-month-old child for an hour and a half.

We had brought some toys with us: a car, a small ball, soft blocks, and a bucket with plastic shape things. The speech therapist also had many toys that we commandeered. Our understanding of Russian orphanage life is that the sheer volume of kids makes it difficult for the staff to give each child the attention he or she deserves. The staff in the Kemerovo orphanage were wonderful with the kids and clearly cared about each child. There were just too many orphans. The typical results for such children are developmental delays and poor social skills.

Little Kiril was happy, engaged, and clearly interested in the world around him. Kiril especially like poking each of our faces. Kiril pleasantly surprised us by the way he interacted with us. He seemed to really enjoy playing with us and was not shy at all. We took some digital pictures[08] for ourselves and for our doctor back in Boston. The time came for us to go, and we left with a positive outlook.

Back at the hotel, I tried to send some of the pictures to the New England Medical Center International Adoption

---

08 A 1-megapixel camera that really helped us in getting a quick report from Boston.

Clinic. Have you ever tried to use the Russian version of Windows? We managed to get off a written report and a picture of Kiril, though I did use some of my new Russian curses. Our doctor called us that night with a list of things to check the next day.

We dined that night with the Irish couple hoping to bring home two toddlers. So far, they had not been to court and were getting exasperated with their agency.

This is the dinner when Elisabeth ordered an entrée described in English as "chicken meat" and was served chicken livers. Elisabeth had a clear look of disgust on her face, and she was not happy. I guess the menu translation lacked a certain level of accuracy, and we lacked an in-depth Russian vocabulary. I enjoyed a lovely chicken-vegetable dinner with a cream sauce.

The nightlife in Kemerovo for foreigners is a little lacking; so is the television show selection. We have resolved to bring a portable DVD player for the second trip (in the hope that cutting edge '90s tech will save our sanity).

September 13, 2005

On this day, we were to see Kiril in the morning and the afternoon. The morning session was short, only about an hour. Kiril was just as happy and curious as the day before. It was a nice visit.

We then went with Irina and the Minnesota couple for a light lunch and to kill some time before the afternoon meeting. Again, not much going on in Kemerovo for foreigners who do not speak Russian. We did stop to buy a large amount of disposable diapers for the orphanage at the request of the director.

OK, now for the marathon three-hour session. We saw Kiril again in the speech therapist's room. We played, laughed, and had a good time. Toward the end, we all got tired. Kiril would then rest on Elisabeth's shoulder. At one point, I lay on the floor, on my back, and Kiril took a short snooze on my chest. The little guy did not want to miss anything, so he would jump awake and then poke me in the face. Finally, it was time to say goodbye. We were tired but a little reluctant to leave.

Later that afternoon, the Minnesota couple asked Irina where they could exchange some more money. Irina had our driver stop on a busy street in the main shopping area. Irina then stated that the black market exchange rate was better than the official bank rate. We stopped in the shopping district not far from the Hotel Kuzbass.

"Those men there can exchange your money," said Irina pointing to some gentlemen congregating nearby.

"Are you sure?" I said, "There are uniformed police standing right by the 'informal' money changers."

Irina stated, "Don't worry so much. The police are

there to protect the money exchangers, not arrest their customers."

"Oh, of course," I replied. Elisabeth gave me a jab and a *look*. The Minnesota couple exchanged money without any trouble or law enforcement involvement. Free enterprise at work in the former Soviet Union.

We dined that night with the Minnesota couple at the same Russian restaurant. Elisabeth went for the relatively safe pork chop, and I tried the beef Stroganoff. We then walked with the Minnesota couple down to the WWII memorial by the Tom River. Another *happenin'* night in Russian coal country. It was time to party like it was 1949.

Irina, in the afternoon, reminded us to meet in the lobby at 6 a.m. the next day to go to the airport. The Minnesota couple was ready to go, but we were not. Our agency had told us to stay an extra day, but nobody had told Irina. Fortunately, Irina handled the late-breaking news with aplomb and was able to arrange for us to see Kiril the next day.

I managed to send two pictures to the adoption clinic in Boston. Our doctor called us at about 1:00 a.m. Kemerovo time and gave us a neutral-to-good report.

"This little guy seems OK," said our doctor. "I do not see any obvious signs of fetal alcohol syndrome, but his ears are placed a little low."

Elisabeth was pleased. "That's a good sign."

Our doctor continued, "His height, weight, and head circumference were all small for his age but fairly typical of Russian babies in orphanages. I wish we had more information, but I would put this boy's risk at having medical issues at 'average' under these circumstances."

Medically, with just scant information, nothing said, "Stop!" so we proceeded.

At about 1:30 a.m., Elisabeth said, "Kiril seems like a great boy. I think we should adopt him."

"I agree, but I'm also nervous. "

"Me, too, honey, but we'll do this together. We make a great team."

We then went back to our respective bolted-to-the-floor twin beds and fell asleep.

September 14, 2005

Except for the telephone call from our doctor in Boston, we both slept through the night, finally.

We had the morning free because the orphanage said to come by about 2 p.m. We ate breakfast at a Japanese restaurant about seven minutes from the hotel. I still do not know what ingredients were in my omelet, but we both liked our meals. Jamestown, in western New York, had no Japanese restaurants in 2005, but Kemerovo, in Siberia, did.

The last visit with Kiril took place in the orphanage's

music room, a room much larger than the speech therapist's room. First, we talked with the orphanage doctor again to follow up on a couple of points our Boston doctor had made. Kiril seemed to recognize us and smiled when they brought him in.

We played and laughed like the other times, but this time, we seemed to make a connection. It was really hard to say goodbye knowing it would be months before we could come back.

After this last visit with Kiril, Irina asked us if we wanted to adopt Kiril.

"So, do you want to adopt Kiril?" asked Irina in a delightfully blunt manner.

Kiril seemed very outgoing and apparently enjoyed meeting Elisabeth and me. We felt Kiril looked and acted relatively healthy for such a small little boy. He seemed to have a good personality. How else do you make such a decision? Elisabeth and I had to make one of the most important decisions of our lives, and of Kiril's, while sitting in the lobby of the Hotel Kuzbass. Elisabeth and I had never been in this position before. Luckily, we had discussed this situation in the middle of the night before Irina asked us.

"Yes, we do," Elisabeth and I said. Irina had us sign some paperwork that formally stated our request to adopt Kiril.

We went back to the Japanese restaurant for dinner. On

our menu: yakitori (chicken on a stick), miso soup, salad, some pork dish, and another chicken dish. I enjoyed a Kirin Lager with dinner. It was all tasty.

Well, we packed that night and set the alarm for 4:50 a.m.

September 15, 2005

Morning came really early. Neither of us felt sorry to leave that sorry hotel room even if it meant another thirty-hour travel day. Irina, really a saint by now, met us at six and took us to the airport in the frosty air. We flew to Moscow with the Wisconsin and Florida couples. They were to spend a few days in Moscow arranging for their children's US visas.

We had to sit in the main economy section for this flight in another TU-154M aircraft. The seats were much closer together, and the entire flight was uncomfortable. Once again, the crew turned up the heat to about 85 degrees. The overall flight was just awful, even though we sort of enjoyed the meal.

In Moscow, Sergei and Viktor met us at the domestic Sheremetyevo terminal and drove us over to the international section. We had a snack with Sergei at a TGI Friday's, and then he bid us *do-svidanya*. We then shopped in duty-free and ate at the Indian restaurant that was out of Indian food. We walked around some more and then went to our gate area.

The flights home were OK for economy class. From Frankfurt to Dulles, we actually sat in the very last row of the airplane. Fortunately, the galley crew served us first, and we did not have to wait for the carts to make their way to us.

Andy picked us up in Buffalo at about 11 p.m. He drove us home, and we got to bed about 1:30 a.m. after some really great showers. At that point, we had been awake for about thirty-two hours.

The next two months were filled with so many things that I wrote a separate chapter. Little did we realize at the time that our marathon trip to Siberia was just the first leg in a much longer, much more trying journey.

Bringing Wallace Home

Our Second Trip to Siberia

The Interlude

After formally requesting to adopt Kiril, Elisabeth and I returned to Jamestown. This marked a very frantic and stressful two months for us. It was also a time of the Second Great Paperwork Chase.

Soon after our first trip, our adoption agency notified us that our dossier had "expired."

"Tom, I have good news and bad news," wrote our agency handler. "You have a court date of November 23. Unfortunately, you need to have all of your documents updated."

"Great and Not Great," I replied.

While Elisabeth and I did not personally feel we had passed our "use by date," apparently the Russian government rules are that prospective adoptive parents' dossiers are good for only one year. Our dossier would expire before we could get back to Kemerovo and pick up

Wallace (whom we then still knew as Kiril). To add to the unbridled fun, we had only about two weeks to complete the new round of paperwork so that all of the documents could be sent to Kemerovo.

Elisabeth and I teamed up and *again* obtained the following documents:

- Updated certifications on our physicals
- Recertified home study reports
- Recertified income verification documents
- Brand-new real property certification
- Update criminal history searches (No, there was nothing to report.)
- My neighbor's lawnmower (It seemed like a good idea.)
- And any other forms that I now forget

One of the most awkward items we had to collect was a copy of our physician's license. The Russian government, really the Kemerovo regional government, apparently believed that some other adoptive parents had presented forged documents in the past. That meant more work for subsequent adoptive parents. Elisabeth cheerfully let me procure this particular document. Fortunately, our doctor, Dr. Liu, lived just a few blocks from our house. We often saw Dr. Liu walking her dog, Bob, in the neighborhood.

"Uh, hi Dr. Liu. How is the doctor business these days?"

After a pause, Dr. Liu responded, "Fine, Tom. I just gave

you another physical. Do you need anything else?"

"Well, yes. The Russian government needs a copy of your doctor's license for our dossier. How about those Red Sox?"

"Huh?!?" replied Dr. Liu.

"It seems that other people, not Elisabeth or I, have presented fake documents in the past. Now everything has to be 'extra verified' including the physician's report you did for us last week."

"OK, no problem. I'll fax it right over."

"Actually, Dr. Liu, can I come by with a notary and make a notarized photocopy?"

"Fine, but I should make you walk Bob for the next week."

All of the forms that we collected were, of course, duly notarized. However, for international use, we had to send every one of these documents to a state office in Albany for apostilles. What is an apostille? It is your state government's certification that the notary publics who notarized your forms are actually notary publics. Basically, for an apostille, you get to pay a modest fee (per form) to your state to doubly certify each form that you present. At least the state of New York puts a fancy seal on each document it apostilles.

Our revised dossier had to travel to Russia about two weeks before our second trip. I had a folder of about ten documents that needed new apostilles and literally only two days to get this done in order to keep our court date in Kemerovo.

However, Albany (New York) is about a six-hour drive from Jamestown, and winter weather had started to arrive in November 2005. I looked at a twelve-hour round-trip drive to get these documents apostiled. Then my partner at our law firm had an idea.

He called the New York Secretary of State like they were best friends (they were not). Andy, my law partner, somehow managed to get the direct phone number for the Secretary of State's office in Albany and got her secretary on the phone.

"Hi, this Andy. How are you today?"

"Fine, Andy. How can I help you?" (Remember, these two people do not know each other.)

"Well, I need to get some documents apostiled tomorrow as part of an international adoption, and I am here in Jamestown. Can you help me?"

"Sure. Let me see what I can do."

The Secretary of State's secretary then connected Andy with the person who processes apostilles. By connect, I mean that there was no voicemail, no "press 1 to continue," or any other bureaucratic techno hurdle.

Andy then spoke to the apostille person and explained the problem. This very nice person gave Andy an address to use for FedEx and told him to tell me to send the documents directly to her with a prepaid return FedEx envelope. I immediately dashed off to the FedEx office at the Jamestown International Airport (oddly enough, you can only fly to Pittsburgh from there, despite its international designation). Thirty-six hours later, I received my documents with shiny new apostille seals on them.

At a time when Elisabeth and I needed a break, we got a huge one, thanks to Andy. What could have been a document nightmare ended with no problems. I sent the documents to our adoption agency in time for us to keep our court date in Kemerovo. You might now realize why Elisabeth and I do not really hold our adoption agency in high regard. They had promised to handle the apostille part of the process, and we ended up doing all of the work.

Though we managed to put together a duly notarized and apostiled dossier in time for our second trip to Kemerovo, Elisabeth and I were beyond anxious. We seriously considered having our priest bless all of the documents, but there was no "blessing of the adoption documents" ceremony in the Episcopal Book of Common Prayer.

Elisabeth and I also had another issue with our adoption agency. Neither of us was pleased with our hotel room on the first trip and even less pleased with our lack of input on the domestic Russian travel arrangements. We did not travel halfway around the world to stay in a hotel room decorated by George Orwell. This time, things would be different.

I made our flight arrangements for the Moscow-Kemerovo-Moscow flights. Aeroflot actually has a decent English language website that explains their flight schedules. I ended up using a US travel website because I could get trip insurance and other U.S. consumer protections.

The only thing I could not do was purchase Wallace's plane ticket to Moscow. We would have to do that in Kemerovo after the formal adoption.

Elisabeth and I had made our hotel reservations while we were in Kemerovo on the first trip. We knew that we had reserved a refurbished suite that promised an actual shower, moveable beds, and a crib.

Our adoption agency, however, fumed and fussed over our travel arrangements. My guess is that their in-country representatives received a commission on the travel arrangements. Elisabeth and I, however, knew that Kiril would be traveling home with us, and we wanted to make sure that our travel arrangements would not make things unnecessarily uncomfortable. Our adoption agency threatened us with more fees for making our own travel arrangements, but we held firm. I am happy to report that our domestic (and international) travel arrangements worked out nicely, and our adoption agency never did charge us additional fees.

One of the other decisions Elisabeth and I had to make was to choose a new name for our son. The hospital staff had chosen the name Kiril. As I mentioned earlier, there was no (apparent) family connection to the name.

At the time of adoption, we had a one-time chance to choose a new name. We chose to name our son Wallace Thomas. Wallace was Elisabeth's father's name, and my father is named Thomas. (Elisabeth vetoed an earlier suggestion of mine: The Dude. Apparently, Elisabeth does not abide.)

Our adoption agency, in the midst of the Second Great Paperwork Chase, was kind enough to tell Elisabeth and me to work even faster on our new dossier. Other things needed to happen as well. We also took some time to finally buy baby furniture and clothes. One of the happiest moments in between our two trips was going to our local big box store and picking out a crib. I think that moment really made the whole adoption process seem real and tangible. (I will skip the part where putting together the crib took several hours and whole year's worth of swearing.)

It also occurred to me that Elisabeth needed a proper baby shower.

I worked with Elisabeth's sister, Tina, to plan a surprise baby shower for her. At that time, Elisabeth and Tina's mother lived in a skilled nursing facility near Jamestown. The facility's director generously let us hold Elisabeth's shower in an activity room at the facility. I was in charge of food and drinks while Tina worked on the invitations. Tina specifically told me that I could *not* spike the punch or serve Spam-based appetizers. Once all the ladies arrived, they invited me to leave and let the party begin. To this day, Elisabeth has not told me what exactly "went down" at her baby shower.

For about the only time in our marriage, I was able to completely surprise Elisabeth. The baby shower turned out to be a smashing success even though it lacked any Spam appetizers. We now possessed enough baby stuff to outfit the Duggar kids. The baby shower was only days before we left for Kemerovo.

We Flew 4,726 Miles to Play Gin Rummy

Like our first trip to Kemerovo, we purchased economy tickets to Moscow. This time, however, we cashed in our United Airlines frequent flyer miles to upgrade to business class. This turned out to be a very good (and comfortable) decision. I cannot emphasize enough the practicality of *not* paying money for your business-class airline tickets.

Our friend Barbara drove us to Buffalo to catch our late afternoon flight to Chicago. To celebrate our trip, Elisabeth and I enjoyed a romantic dinner in the United concourse of O'Hare International Airport. And by *romantic*, I mean:

"Do we have enough diapers?" Elisabeth pondered out loud.

While noshing on a quesadilla appetizer, I replied, "If not, we'll buy some in Russia. What about feeding Wallace?"

"I packed eating utensils for the baby and some bottles. We'll have to buy baby food in Kemerovo and Moscow." It may not have been the most romantic discussion ever, but Elisabeth and I felt giddy with excitement. We had waited through years of sadness to have a conversation like this.

We traveled over to Kemerovo during Thanksgiving week. Our transatlantic flight was not very crowded at all. According to Elisabeth, United served better tasting wine on this flight as compared to our first trip two months previous. In Frankfurt, I partook of another $11 stale donut & Diet Coke pick-me-up. This time, the donut tasted only slightly stale, but I still felt like a sophisticated business traveler. Then on to Moscow.

Our stay in Moscow lasted about twelve painfully boring hours. Here is a list of things you can do at Sheremetyevo Airport while waiting for your connecting flight to Siberia:

- Play gin rummy with your wife and win. This strategy is recommended for anyone looking to placate their wife with wine sold at a Russian airport.
- Play gin rummy with your wife and lose. Your wife might then get you a $5 bottle of water.
- Pinch yourself: the return trip home will be with our son.
- Practice your rudimentary Russian at a restaurant and end up ordering sandwiches of undetermined origin.
- *Sleeping* in the world's most uncomfortable chair that is bolted to the floor. The people who designed our first hotel room in Kemerovo went on to work on the Sheremetyevo Airport project.
- *Not* annoying the well-armed security staff.
- Trying to blot from your mind the fact that there was a cleaning lady in the men's room who had interesting views on privacy.
- Realize that Sergei, your driver/translator, knows more about the NBA than you do.

After very little sleep, very little bathing, and a serving of communist-era beef Stroganoff, we boarded our flight to Kemerovo. In 2005, domestic Aeroflot flights were not that expensive. We had hoarded enough rubles to fly business class for this flight as well. Of course Aeroflot was still using the TU-154M on this route. It is with great relief that I report that our third flight on a Soviet era aircraft proved uneventful. The flight crew still kept the cabin at a balmy 85 degrees, but we were packed like a small group of cattle instead of shoulder-to-shoulder sardines. We arrived in Kemerovo fresh and dandy as you might expect.

Kemerovo Was Our Most Visited Foreign City in 2005

Our guide and translator from our first trip, Irina, met us at the airport. It takes a special person to go to the airport at 6:00 a.m. on a cold November morning in order to pick up two *fresh and dandy* Americans. Like herding zombies, Irina escorted us to a waiting minivan.

Kemerovo's weather in November has all the charm and warmth as you might imagine of Siberia in the early winter. Our flight landed before dawn, and we felt the cold wind slap us across our faces. Elisabeth and I were so excited about adopting Wallace that thought we were in Siberian Disneyland. We were also quite tired and eager to freshen up or at least change out of clothes that we had worn for about forty straight hours.

The Hotel Kuzbass Is Located at 20 Vesennaya Street

The Hotel Kuzbass indeed looked a sight for sore eyes. Our prior planning paid off in that we were able to check in at 6:45 in the morning, and the hotel staff managed to give us a refurbished room that had new furniture and an actual shower (Elisabeth and I worked directly with Irina versus trusting our adoption agency to make all of the right travel choices for us). We also chose a suite this time so that we were not all bunched up in a tiny rom.

The Hotel Kuzbass gave us what they called a "Comfort Suite." We had a very nice living room that included a couch, coffee table, dinner table, and chairs. Our bathroom fixtures were clearly modern and lacked any Khrushchev-era influences. We no longer felt like we were visiting the 1950s-era Soviet Union. The bedroom was separated from the living room by double doors and came with two luxurious twin beds. Elisabeth and I felt like Rob and Laura in the *Dick Van Dyke Show*. What married couple sleeps in separate beds in the same bedroom?[09] At least these beds were not bolted to the floor, and Elisabeth and I shoved the beds together (though Irina nervously admonished us to separate them again before we checked out!).

---

09 Because Jamestown is the hometown of Lucile Ball, I should mention that Lucy and Ricky also slept in twin beds.

This brings to mind another charming misadventure. One morning, while at the Hotel Kuzbass, Elisabeth was getting ready in the bathroom. I closed the lid on the toilet and sat to talk with Elisabeth about the upcoming day's events. The toilet lid then cracked and broke. I then had the embarrassing duty to explain to the floor matron, with Irina's slightly exasperated help, how I managed to break the toilet lid. The hotel charged us about $10 and gave me a very stern warning about damaging hotel property. Elisabeth still teases me about this twelve years after the incident.

Before we leave the Hotel Kuzbass, I have one other strange incident to report. During both our first and second trips, I (not Elisabeth) received interesting phone calls at the Hotel Kuzbass. Not long after we checked in each time, the phone in our room rang. I happen to answer each time. A woman spoke to me in accented English:

"Would you like the services of a beautiful Russian woman for the evening?"

I replied in the only way I knew how, "Uhhhhhh, Uhhhhhh, no thank you!" and hung up the phone like it glowed with prurient radioactivity.

Red faced, I immediately told Elisabeth about the calls each time they happened. Thankfully, Elisabeth understood that our mere presence in the hotel probably generated the phone calls. Elisabeth was just as understanding the other days when we got other phone calls offering me a chance to *relax* with a beautiful Russian woman.

In no way to I condone prostitution or the mistreatment of women. I, however, do want to accurately report what happened while we were in Russia. These phone calls were so out of the ordinary for us but still a part of our Russian experience. These things just do not happen in Jamestown, New York.

Irina Was a Taskmaster and an Angel

After showers and naps, Elisabeth and I were ready to go see Kiril. We all piled into the minivan ("mini" being the key part), and we headed off to the orphanage. The orphanage director allowed a short visit with Kiril, which we enjoyed. Irina, however, was eager to get us started on the Great Kemerovo Paper Chase. Imagine going to the DMV several times per day, but everyone speaks only Russian. That was our life for a few days.

First, we had to go to the Kemerovo Family Court to submit some paperwork. Then we had to go start the paperwork to get Kiril a passport. Next, we went to some other government office to drop off some different paperwork. Lastly, we had to go to the local Aeroflot office to make a reservation for Kiril to fly to Moscow with us using our reservation. The Aeroflot office at least smelled nice.

It is a blur to me now about all the places we went. Irina, though, gave us some very good advice.

"In two days, you and Elisabeth must go to Kemerovo Family Court to appear before a judge and make your case to adopt Kiril. Everyone adopting must do this, even Russians."

Elisabeth said, "Yes, our adoption agency in Florida told us. We also heard about court from other parents who adopted from Russia."

"You must understand that the judge will want Tom to talk first and then ask him questions. In Russian family court, the husband always talks first. After that, then the judge will ask Elisabeth to speak."

Normally, Elisabeth and I would have made a joint presentation. However, we inferred from Irina that this was not the time to bring American views on gender equality into a Russian courtroom. When in Rome, eat Italian food; when in Kemerovo, listen to Irina.[10]

Our short talk with Irina got me going on preparing my opening statement. I wanted to start with: "Hey, you guys make a good borscht here!" or "What's the deal with Putin on horseback? I'll be here all week! Be good to your waitresses." Elisabeth stated something about neutering should I actually open with those lines. I went back to

---

10 I think I correctly used a semicolon in that sentence.

work and came up with something more appropriate to the situation.

Thursday morning came, and Elisabeth and I felt as you might expect: ready to regurgitate everything we had ever eaten. You may have heard of the term "nervous wreck." Amplify term about thousand times, and you may understand how we felt. Irina and our driver picked us up at about 9:00 a.m. The minivan still felt quite mini. We made it over to the Kemerovo Family Court and promptly started to wait. And wait some more.

Our court date took place in the eon before the advent of smartphones and tablet computers. We could not rescue angry birds, take selfies, or update our social media statuses. I had also lived a smoke-free life until this point, but I seriously contemplated taking up chain smoking as the wait continued. I think Elisabeth could have knitted a tarp if she knew how to knit. Finally, they called our case. (We had actually waited only thirty minutes, but I aged about ten years in that time.)

The called us into the world's smallest and utilitarian courtroom.[11] Seated at the head of the conference table was the family court judge. To our left was a government social worker. To our right was an advocate for prospective adoptive children. Sitting with Elisabeth and me was an

---

11 Though the town justice in French Creek, New York, used to hold court in his dining room.

official government interpreter who was quite nice. Never underestimate the skill it takes to simultaneously translate one language into another. (Irina, not a government employee, had to stay in the hallway.)

The judge started the proceedings, introduced the other people, and then asked me why we wanted to adopt Kiril. I know I spoke for some time and said many things that I do not now remember. The emotion of the morning really impairs my memory of my actual presentation. I probably talked about Elisabeth and me, our stay in infertility Hell, our jobs, our parenting philosophy, and our desire to adopt young Kiril. When I was done, no one had any questions.

The judge did not ask Elisabeth to speak for more than a couple of minutes. The judge then asked us all to leave the room. Normally, as an attorney, I would view this as an "Oh, crap!" moment. A judge that asks you to leave her courtroom is usually not a happy judge.

Thankfully, Irina and our interpreter had told us in advance what to expect. Foreign adoptions in Russia are the fastest court proceedings ever. The judge asked us to leave so she could deliberate. While the judge deliberated, the interpreter and social worker stated that they had never been in an adoption proceeding where there were no questions. Apparently, I had covered nearly everything in my opening statement, and Elisabeth filled in whatever I had missed. By no means am I a modern Clarence

Darrow. For whatever reason, on that particular day, and at that particular time, I managed to say all the right things without sounding like a jackass. Any attorney in Jamestown will tell you that this has not happened to me since then.

Five minutes later, we were summoned back into the courtroom. (I think the "courtroom" doubled as a lunch room.) The judge smiled and told us she had approved us to adopt Kiril, who would now be known as Wallace Thomas Rankin. Elisabeth and I got all teary eyed as we thanked the judge and everyone else. Irina, however, had no time for tears of joy.

Irina collected the paperwork we needed and ushered us out of the courtroom. We then boarded our suddenly spacious minivan and headed for the next round of paperwork. We had to get a new birth certificate for Wallace. We needed to pick up his passport. We needed to get another form of some sort. Finally, we had all of the documents but the passport. That would take another day.

No Green Bean Casserole but Still an Amazing Thanksgiving

Only after chasing all of this paper did we go pick up Wallace. This would be the last time we would go to the orphanage. We brought some new clothes for Wallace. Our understanding of pickup day was that all of Wallace's clothes from the orphanage would stay at there. Wallace was fourteen months old when we became one family.

Elisabeth and I also figured out for the first time just how small Wallace was for his age. We knew he was small, but did not realize how small. The twelve-month-size clothes we picked out for Wallace left him enough room to fit in an oven-roasted turkey. We determined later that Wallace was about the size of a nine-month-old even though he was fourteen months.

Think of your favorite happy song. That was how we felt as we all boarded the once-again terribly mini minivan for the ride back to the Hotel Kuzbass. I have never seen Elisabeth so happy as the day we picked up Wallace at the orphanage. Within twenty-four hours, we would be tested as parents.

First, though, we had to get used to having a child in our hotel room. The Hotel Kuzbass let us borrow a crib. The orphanage staff said that Wallace did nap in the afternoon. We put Wallace in the crib, and he sat there and stared at us. All three of us were unsure what to do. Wallace went from a room full of kids and noise to a quiet hotel room with two funny-looking (funny-smelling?) adults.

Feeding time turned out to be an adventure in adaptation. The Hotel Kuzbass had no high chairs for young guests. Wallace made it very clear to us when he wanted to eat. Irina took us to a store to get a small supply of baby food.

However, we had no microwave oven. The tap water was quite hot, and Elisabeth made some warmish cereal mixed with fruit puree (Irina chided us for mixing these and - to this day - we do not know why). I held Wallace in my lap while Elisabeth fed him. If she did not feed fast enough, Wallace bellowed. We learned very quickly that Wallace is a boy who likes his food served lukewarm and served fast.

Eventually, Wallace took a nap. Elisabeth and I were just exhausted, both emotionally and physically. Fast forward to dinnertime: It was still Thursday—Thanksgiving Day in the USA. Thanksgiving Day forever changed for the Rankin family because this is the day we became a family of three.

Elisabeth and I also learned the joys of changing diapers. Wallace actually seemed happy to accommodate us when we had to change him. Clearly the orphanage staff had trained Wallace to not give them a hard time about diaper changes. The only thing odd was the foul-smelling deposits in his diapers. I mean foul. We learned more about these deposits when we got back to Jamestown.

It was a very cold night in Kemerovo, and our dining options were suddenly limited. Neither of us wanted to take Wallace outside just to go to a restaurant. So, I bundled up and went outside to get some dinner for all of us. The closest takeout place was not too far, The Golden Chicken, but it offered only fried chicken and the menu was in

Russian. Irina had warned us not eat chicken because of some type of bird flu.

Using my patented "point and use crappy Russian" communication skills, I managed to get two chicken dinners.

(I have *italicized* the parts of the conversation that were in Russian. That means I am really guessing at what the person was saying, including me.)

"*Next!*"

"Hi, can I have two chicken breast dinners with French fries? By the way, is your chicken free-range chicken?"

"*I don't know what you are saying. Please point on the menu.*"

"*Umm, two orders of deep fried socks please.*"

"*Hey, you: Just point. I'll figure out the rest.*"

(Pointing) "*Two orders of raw chicken please.*"

"*OK, but how about I cook it for you?*"

(Smiling) "*OK!*"

"*Drinks?*"

"*No, I don't need an oil change.*"

"*OK, no drinks. You will get water at your hotel.*"

I am happy to report that no member of the Rankin family contracted any avian flu or *Stalin's Revenge* from that dinner. This was possibly the worst fried chicken dinner known to mankind, but Elisabeth and I were so happy that we would have eaten marinated sawdust that night. Our first Thanksgiving as a complete family was eating oddly fried chicken in our hotel room in Kemerovo, Siberia. And then the fun ended for a few days.

Wallace woke up the next morning with a low fever (Irina was certain that this was because we mixed his cereal with jars of fruit). I forget if we all went to get his passport and Aeroflot ticket or if I went alone with Irina. At any rate, by late afternoon, it was clear that Master Wallace was quite feverish—about 103 degrees. Irina left and brought back the orphanage pediatrician. It was interesting to see Wallace's face brighten when she spoke Russian to him. The pediatrician did not think Wallace had a serious illness but said he might not be able to fly with us tomorrow to Moscow.

Elisabeth and I were slightly frantic in part because of how Irina described the likely scenario should Wallace have been admitted to a local hospital. [The name, "Wallace", caused some difficulties for Russians speaking to us in English.]

"If Uaallace has fever, then the hospital will keep him for about seven to ten days."

"Really?" we both exclaimed. "In the U.S., we would be surprised if a child was admitted to a hospital with only a fever. Even then, it would be for one or two days."

"It is different here. You would not really be able to see Uaallace while he is in the hospital except for short visiting hour."

"Seven to ten days?!?"

"Yes."

"What can we do to avoid the hospital tonight?"

Elisabeth and I really did not want to spend an extra ten days in Kemerovo while our son recovered from a fever of unknown origin.

Thus began the Night of No Sleep. The orphanage pediatrician gave Irina a prescription for some medications, and Irina filled it for us. Unfortunately, the medication instructions were in Russian. Irina tried to explain to us what to do, but we did not fully understand how to administer the meds. That may seem odd, but remember that we had absolutely no teaspoons (the instructions most likely listed the recommended dosages in milliliters, but we had no milliliter measuring spoon either) or measuring cups, and the instructions were printed in Russian. After Irina left, we basically guessed at the right dosages for Wallace.

Irina called later, and Wallace was still feverish. Irina, not caring for herself, came over and called paramedics. It was about 12:30 a.m. at this point, and we were determined to go to Moscow later in the morning. The paramedics stated the same thing as the orphanage pediatrician: Wallace did not have a serious illness but that he might not be able to fly with us to Moscow in seven hours unless his fever went down. One of the paramedics suggested we give Wallace an alcohol rub every twenty minutes. And by alcohol, the paramedic meant vodka. Really, he said use vodka.

So, at 1:00 a.m., Irina and I braved the bitterly cold Siberian wind and went to an all-night convenience store about four blocks from the Hotel Kuzbass. This marked the first of many times that I would mutter, "I hope Wallace appreciates this when he gets older!" There I purchased a bottle of vodka for about $1. Calling this stuff horrid is a disservice to that word. We then trudged back to the Hotel Kuzbass.

Irina said good night and promised to pick us up at around 5:30 a.m. For the next four hours or so, at twenty-minute intervals, Elisabeth and I would rub Wallace with the world's worst vodka. We would all then nap for twenty minutes. As happy as Elisabeth and I were, we were also miserable. Wallace was not too happy about the situation either and was not shy in voicing his opinion about the whole "quit rubbing vodka on my naked body" situation. In the end, the vodka martini rub worked. Wallace had only a very slight temperature by 5:30 a.m.

The Doctor's Elevator Did Not Go to the Top Floor

The business class section of our flight to Moscow was fairly empty and quiet. Wallace enjoyed the flight—he got to sleep without the indignity of waking up every twenty minutes to have some stranger rub vodka on his torso. Elisabeth and I did not sleep so much because it sounded like our ancient airliner was dropping parts all the way from Kemerovo to Moscow. However, we all made it safely to Moscow and the Marriott Hotel. Then the medical hilarity continued.

Wallace was still running a low-grade fever, and we wanted to know what was wrong with our little guy. Our new interpreter, Bob, made some calls and got us an appointment with a clinic run by a US-trained physician. Elisabeth felt completely exhausted and wanted to stay at our hotel. So, I took Martini Wallace on what I thought would be an uneventful trip. But uneventful turned out to mean the most annoying four hours of my life.

Late November brings cold weather to Moscow, just like Kemerovo. That meant that Wallace and I had to bundle up in just about every scrap of clothing we had. I looked like a woolen blimp. I also brought his diaper bag that Elisabeth had thoughtfully packed with diapers, wipes, extra clothes, and several pounds of lead weights.

The two of us then jumped in a taxi and went to the clinic.

We arrived at the clinic, I paid the driver, and Wallace and I ungracefully exited the taxi. I also had to exit the taxi while holding Wallace and his ten-pound diaper bag. I do not remember the check-in procedure at the clinic, but I do remember that the elevator stopped with two flights of stairs remaining to the examination room. At this point, Wallace and I had shed our protective woolen space suits because it was about 80 degrees in the clinic. We exited the elevator and then began a forced march up two flights of stairs.

The nurse did not offer to carry anything, so I was compelled to carry Wallace, his now-twenty-five-pound diaper bag, one large woolen space suit, and one tiny woolen space suit up two flights of stairs and down a long hallway. I was about ready to revisit my Aeroflot breakfast by the time we got to the examining room.

At least the doctor was there waiting for us. The doctor readily examined Wallace and conversed with me in excellent English.

"Your son has a fever."

I was still recovering from the forced march in sauna-like conditions and wanted to tell the doctor to @#$% ^&*!.

Instead, I said, "Hmmm, that's what I thought, too."

"Have you given Uaallace any medications?"

I pulled out the prescription medications we received in Kemerovo.

"We tried this medicine but did not really know what we were doing."

The doctor then maligned me for not following the directions, which were written in a language that I did not understand.[12]

The doctor then explained to me the dosages, the timetable for our medications, and gave me a plastic cup marked with milliliters. He next said he wanted Wallace to take one more medication for his fever. He pulled out a foil-covered object from the cabinet. I suddenly felt the impending doom of having to do something really gross.

"Uaallace should take a suppository for his fever."

The doctor showed me, umm, how to give the medication to Wallace. With a gleam in his eye he said, and I swear this is true:

"Just plug it in!"[13]

It was at this point that the Dr. Seuss book *Oh, The Places You'll Go* came to mind but in a less metaphorical kind of way.

The doctor then gave me some more suppositories to

---

12 What does, "Дозировка: 20 мл дважды в день" mean? What does, "Никогда не вмешиваться в сухопутной войны в Азии" mean?

13 My apologies to Dave Barry.

give Wallace, once per day. That ended the examination, but the doctor wanted to see if Wallace's fever would respond to the *directly given* medication. The nurse then had Wallace and me wait in the lobby of the building. That meant Dad the Sherpa had another stroll with Wallace, his now-fifty-pound diaper bag, and two woolen space suits. We eventually made it to the lobby.

We both sat on a relatively comfortable bench and relaxed for a few minutes. A nurse brought me a cup of water. After Wallace puked all over my legs, his fever started to go down.

The nurse then called a taxi, and we settled in for a nice long wait while the taxi proceeded to get lost finding the clinic. Wallace was sort of grumpy at this point, and I was a hot, puke-covered, mess. Wallace and I finally made it back to our hotel. Elisabeth asked how things went at the clinic.

"Fine," I said. "The doctor spoke English. He examined Wallace and pronounced our son ill with a fever. The doctor then explained how to administer the medicine we got in Kemerovo."

"OK. Great. Anything else?"

"Yes," I said with a mischievous smile. "The doctor also gave us some special medicine, and only mothers can administer it to children."

"What?"

"That's right. Only mothers can give these special suppositories to their children."

"Oh, no. We will be sharing that duty."

We duly administered the medicines to Wallace, and he quickly returned to health. Thus ended the medical hilarity until we returned to New York.

Bob the interpreter called us the next day and said that we had an appointment at the US embassy. However, the US government mandated that all children adopted outside the states must have a HIV/AIDS test. Bob had arranged for all of us to go to a special clinic for Wallace to get his. More taxis, more woolen space suits.

The staff at this clinic did not speak English and were trained in Russia. Bob came with us and told us that only one parent could go with Wallace to get the test. By the way, Bob said, a nurse would have to draw blood for the test. I volunteered to go with Wallace and be the mean parent.

I remember going down a hallway into a sort of dark room. It really felt like a scene out of the movie *Brazil* except that Robert De Niro never rescued us. The nurse and assistant motioned me to undress Wallace. They then showed me how to hold Wallace for the blood draw. Unfortunately for Wallace, I had to hold his legs in such a way that his tiny *tuchus* was prominently displayed for the nurse. Oh, the indignity of it all. I felt bad for Wallace.

FINDING WALLACE!

The next sound we all heard was Wallace screaming, well, bloody murder. I can only think of how I would feel if some strange people with cold hands stuck a big needle in *my* butt. It is fair to say that Wallace was very unhappy at this point. The nurse finished, and I quickly dressed my decidedly angry son. Wallace was all too happy to get away from me, and go to Elisabeth, once we reunited. By the way, the test results were negative, which was a big positive for Wallace—and a huge relief for us.

We had compiled a large set of freshly minted, Russian government-issued papers at this point. Bob the interpreter announced that we were ready to go to the US embassy after lunch to get Wallace's visa.

The US embassy in Moscow is a large compound taking up about a whole city block. After a thorough security examination, the US security staff let us enter the embassy. There were a whole bunch of adoptive parents with us, and a staff person escorted us through a labyrinth of hallways that only M.C. Escher could have loved. Our group finally arrived in a very bland but secure office that resembled a bank lobby.

The staff gave each family a number, as if we were waiting to get half a pound of salami at the local deli. In due course, a pleasant woman called us to her window. The foreign service officer was very nice and gentle. Of course she sat behind about two inches of bulletproof glass, and

I suspected the surrounding walls were fortified against most known explosives.

"Mr. and Mrs. Rankin."

We walked to the window.

"Hi, we are the Rankins," Elisabeth said.

"Congratulations! OK. Everything seems to be in order."

The foreign service officer then stamped some forms and processed our paperwork very efficiently. She next affixed a US visa into Wallace's Russian passport. She then gave us a large sealed envelope filled with papers.

"Here is Wallace's passport, and your other papers are in this envelope that I have sealed. Under no circumstances are you to open this envelope. You must hand it to the airport immigration officer when you land back in the USA. Good luck!"

"Thank you!" both Elisabeth and I replied.

This really was a pleasant and simple appointment notwithstanding the very heavy security in the embassy. We knew in advance to expect this envelope. We then left the Escher-like catacombs of the US embassy and returned to our hotel.

Vietnam Airlines Flight Crews Stay at the Moscow Marriott

Our flight home was not until two days after we picked up Wallace's visa. With Wallace still not feeling 100 percent and the outside temperature hovering below freezing, Elisabeth and I elected to stay in the hotel. I do remember one way we entertained Wallace was to put him in his stroller and walk up and down the hallways of our hotel.

We also made up a song to help Wallace get used to his new name. To the tune of the Flintstones theme song, it goes like this:

Wallace, Wallace Thomas, happiest boy in this whole house.

Wallace, Wallace Thomas, you sleep quieter than a mouse.

That's right, we're the Rankin family and live on a very bumpy street.

You'll be friends with every one you meet.

Wallace, Wallace Thomas, happiest boy in this whole house.

For trips in the car, we modified the lyrics:

Wallace, Wallace Thomas, happiest boy in this whole car.

Wallace, Wallace Thomas, with your smile and laugh

you'll go far.[14]

Elisabeth and I started singing this to Wallace at our hotel in Moscow, and we still sing it to him today. Now a big tough twelve-year-old, Wallace is mortified when we dare sing this song.

I also remember one other thing about this short interlude. We managed to find the only Indian restaurant in Moscow that A) had staff that spoke English and B) would deliver. One of our last meals in Moscow was a lovely Indian dinner complete with warm nan bread.

The night before we were to fly home, Bob the interpreter came to our hotel to check on us. He asked if we still had the sealed envelope. I nonchalantly told Bob that we had opened it. The look of horror on Bob's face was priceless, but I quickly told him that I was joking. The envelope remained sealed and under locked guard. Bob then swore at me in Russian and relaxed. He promised to pick us up the next morning.

Bright and early the next day, Bob gathered our family of three and drove us for the last time to Sheremetyevo Airport. I was sort of sad that I would never again sit in the world's most uncomfortable chairs while eating prepackaged food of indeterminate origin.

Thornton Wilder is credited with saying, "All good

---

14 Elisabeth and I fully realize that our career in the music industry will be quite limited.

things must come to an end, but bad things can continue forever."[15] Sheremetyevo Airport has remained in service for a long, long time.

The flights from Moscow to Frankfurt and Frankfurt to Dulles were delightfully calm. Thanks to our United Airlines miles, we had plenty of room in business class for all three of us. Wallace flew as a lap baby and did not cry all that much. The worst part was the very long day.

US airlines have their faults, but at least their airplanes are new enough not to qualify for *Antiques Roadshow*.

We landed at Dulles and perked up. At least Elisabeth and I did. Wallace, he was a bit "meh" at this point. US law (in 2005) said that foreign adopted children become US citizens when they enter the USA at the same time as their adoptive American parents. With great excitement, we handed over Wallace's sealed envelope and our passports to the immigration/passport control officer at Dulles.

The immigration officer first confirmed that our hideous passport pictures bore some resemblance to us. She then dared to open Wallace's sealed envelope. Apparently, all of our paperwork arrived in order because the immigration officer next stamped all of our passports with the standard

15 http://www.searchquotes.com/quotation/All_good_things_must_come_to_an_end%2C_but_all_bad_things_can_continue_forever./9688/, last visited on February 25, 2017. Mr. Wilder also apparently said, "If I wasn't an actor, I would be a secret agent."

Dulles arrival stamp. Poof! Wallace became a US citizen! We collected our passports and went to claim our luggage. (We received Wallace's naturalization certificate about a month later).

Customs control was no bother. I guess we did not look like smugglers, though we still had Wallace's Russian medications. We made it to the gate for our connecting flight to Buffalo. This time, we flew on the world's tiniest commuter jet. There was just enough room for all of us in two very cramped seats. Wallace was a very good little traveler. As soon as we were settled on the airplane, we all fell asleep only to wake up as we were taxiing to our gate in Buffalo.

Elisabeth's cousin Lenny met us in Buffalo and gave us a hearty welcome. Elisabeth's brother, Petter (who uses the Swedish spelling of his name), then arrived with his four-wheel drive vehicle. It was December 1, and it was snowing hard in Buffalo and Jamestown. It was a good thing we still had our woolen space suits. More of our family met us at home after the ninety-minute drive from the airport. It was so great to be home. Then the medical hilarity continued.

Our Return from Russia—An Epilogue of Sorts

We arrived in Jamestown on a dark and stormy night in December. There was about four inches of fresh snow on the ground when we got home. Wallace got to meet his Aunt Robin and Aunt Tina. Then we all crashed for about six hours. Jet lag is as fun and sexy as cleaning your gutters.

Before we left for our second trip to Russia, Elisabeth and I had scheduled an appointment for Wallace to meet his new pediatrician the same week we returned. Our trusty Subaru took the Rankin family to Wallace's pediatrician about thirty-six hours after we came home from Russia. Elisabeth called to confirm the appointment after our arrival, and the staff informed us that we would need to bring with us a stool sample from Wallace. That little bit of completely un-fun activity turned out to be very important (but, sometimes, this parenting stuff can be really gross…).

Wallace's pediatrician, "Dr. BT,"[16] was very experienced and had worked with foreign-adopted babies in the past. He was not surprised at all that Wallace was significantly

---

16 Dr. BT is retired now, and I respect his privacy.

underweight. Dr. BT told us that Wallace could eat as much as he wants and to let Wallace decide when he was full. Babies and young children actually have a remarkable ability to self-regulate their food intake.

Dr. BT started Wallace on a crash inoculation schedule, although he said it would take a couple of years for Wallace to fully catch up on his entire vaccination/inoculation regimen. You may remember that we had absolutely no information about Wallace's medical history. We knew more about the president's annual physicals than Wallace's medical history at this point. Dr. BT recommended that we assume Wallace had not received any vaccinations, and Elisabeth and I agreed.

Wallace had to suffer another blood test, and he quite capably voiced his displeasure at having another needle jab after suffering his first vaccinations. The young man clearly did not enjoy this part of his doctor visit. The nurse gave Wallace a sticker for being a good patient. Wallace tried to eat it.

What about the stool sample? Well, the next day, a nurse from Dr. BT's office called to inform us that Wallace had a case of giardia. Due to our newfound ability to carry Wallace's poop to the doctor's office, we learned that Wallace had brought this intestinal parasite with him from Russia. This helped explain Wallace's low weight and horrifically smelling diapers. The medical hilarity continued. Russia does not have an exclusive claim on giardia. You can find this willing parasite all over the world.

Dr. BT's office sent over a script to our local pharmacy. A course of this medicine would cure Wallace of his giardia illness. The key part of the medicine was having it in liquid form because Wallace was far too young to swallow pills. Finding this medicine turned out to be a small scavenger hunt in metropolitan Jamestown. Our family pharmacist informed me that A) he did not carry this giardia medicine and B) his corporate office would not even let him order the stuff.

Our family pharmacist, Bob (his actual name!), is a very nice person. We still use his pharmacy today. Bob courteously called the Monolithic Corporate Pharmacy in town, but they did not/would not carry this medicine Wallace really needed. Our family pharmacist then recommended that I try the only compounding pharmacy in metropolitan Jamestown.

Wallace and I donned our woolen space suits and drove over to our local compounding pharmacy, which is one that mixes combinations of drugs for patients who cannot normally get their medications through regular pharmacies. Think of compounding pharmacies as microbreweries in a corporate pharma world.

I brought in the script, and the pharmacy tech promptly disappeared into the back room. I was getting seriously depressed at this point. Thoughts of driving seventy-five miles (ninety minutes) to Buffalo for one prescription crowded my head and woolen space suit. The thought of continued extra foul diapers did not help either. After some type of really deep conversation with his superior, the pharmacy tech came back out.

The compounding pharmacy carried the medicine Wallace needed. The big talk in the back room was what flavor to make the liquid. The pharmacist intended to take the powder or pill form of the medicine and concoct by hand the liquid form. He wanted to make sure Wallace would drink the stuff so he asked the pharmacy tech to consult with me.

I wanted to say, "How the @#% would I know what flavor Wallace prefers for his medications? He just finished with a course of suppositories for Pete's sake!"

Instead, I calmly asked, "What are the flavor choices?" Wallace and I pondered the situation and chose grape flavor. Actually, I just flipped a coin. Apparently, this was the correct choice because Wallace cheerfully took his handmade giardia medicine.

The day after our trip to pharmacy adventure land, Elisabeth and I received a telephone call from the county health department. "Did we know that Wallace had giardia?" the health worker asked? I replied that we had known this for about a day and that Wallace was now taking medicine for giardia. The health worker seemed greatly relieved and hung up. We never heard from her again, and Wallace recovered nicely from his infection.

There Cannot Be a Happy Ending until the Story Is Over

Once Wallace recovered from giardia, his overall health quickly improved. Over the next two years, Elisabeth and I were obligated to send semiannual reports back to Russia. Part of the process required us to have a visit from a licensed social worker. The social worker then attached her report to go along with ours.

Now, this is where things turned sketchy again. About three months after we brought Wallace home, our main contact at our adoption agency abruptly left. Our agency assigned a new person to help us. We heard from this person only once. After that, we learned that not only had our adoption agency closed but the intermediary agency in Atlanta had filed for bankruptcy.

The name of this intermediary agency was Amrex. A search of "Amrex bankruptcy" on the Internet should reveal that Amrex filed for bankruptcy in 2006. Amrex's bankruptcy petition apparently stated that its debts had exceeded two million dollars. Sadly, Amrex had collected fees from hundreds of prospective parents who never got back their money.

Amrex owed Elisabeth and me about $400 in rebates for when we submitted our post-adoption reports along with other parents who had adopted in late 2005. We never got our money either, but we did not care about that. Wallace was safely home with us.

Elisabeth and I did run into some trouble with our post-adoption reports. Our adoption agency was to send our post-adoption reports to Amrex, who would translate them into Russian and send them to Kemerovo for us. Elisabeth and I wanted to comply but did not know what to do. Eventually, a legitimate adoption agency took over this process. Once they showed us that they were truly legitimate, Elisabeth and I sent our post-adoption reports to this new agency. I look back at our lives in 2004 through 2007 and feel so amazed that the adoption process went so smoothly when we could have ended up in so many pitfalls.

And Then Ten Years Later

Looking back, clear signs existed to show that Wallace was a boy with special needs. Elisabeth and I did not really see these indicators at the time, but others did. Thankfully, some people really cared about our son. Elisabeth was able to take some time off for parental leave but eventually had to return to work. We found a daycare facility for Wallace. He eventually moved on to kindergarten, and we did not see the staff at the daycare place anymore.

About ten years after we brought Wallace home, Elisabeth went to a ceremony for the dedication of a new park in Jamestown. One of the ladies who worked in the baby room at Wallace's old daycare facility saw Elisabeth and approached her.

"Elisabeth, it's nice to see you. How old is Wallace now?"

"Hi, Nancy. It's been a long time. It is great to see you. Can you believe that Wallace is ten now?

"I cannot believe that! I remember when you brought this tiny baby to us."

"He's not so tiny anymore."

"How is Wallace? I knew he was a special child from the first day"

"Really?"

"We never told you this before, but for the first few weeks, all Wallace would do is crawl under the highchairs and hide. He was so scared. Of course we held him and played with him as much as possible."

"My gosh.[17] I never knew this."

"As he moved to the other rooms at the daycare, the teachers would look out for Wallace. We really cared for him. I could just see this little boy struggling in life."

And then Nancy gave Elisabeth and me one of the nicest compliments we have ever received. "We all thought

---

17 Yes, that is an actual expression we both use.

that you and Tom were great parents for Wallace."

Elisabeth and I do not ever hold out ourselves as Parents of the Year. We have struggled with Wallace and made many mistakes. Once in a while, however, a nice compliment can really make our day.

In a few pages, I will describe the not entirely positive way Wallace left this daycare facility. This makes Nancy's conversation with Elisabeth even more special to us. We never knew the full impact of Wallace's time at this facility.

Our three-person family learned to adapt to each other. It soon became apparent that Wallace was special in many ways. The next chapters explain how we came to understand Wallace's special needs as well as our life as a family. There are happy times and sad times like any life story. Wallace's story, though, is about the challenges of life while living with mental illness.

Happily Ever After—The First Few Years

One of the goals of this book is to talk about what happens in a family after the foreign adoption is complete and the child has joined the family. In more personal terms, the process of adopting Wallace was an adventure with a very happy ending. The story, however, does not end with the triumphant return to Jamestown from Russia. That was the beginning of an odyssey that no one in our family could have predicted.[18] What happened over the next few years has been both rewarding and, at times, very difficult.

I wrote this next part of this book for two reasons. First, for other parents of newly adopted children to feel less isolated. The task of integrating an adopted child into a family differs significantly from bringing home a birth child. I do not present this information as a blueprint for success but rather to show what worked for us and what did not.

Second, Elisabeth and I did not know that we had started on the path to a diagnosis of reactive attachment disorder (RAD). How we got there and why we did not get

---

18 I will let you know if we get to an island with a cyclops on it.

the diagnosis sooner is part of our story.

Wallace Was Scared of Taking a Bath

Elisabeth and I are first-time parents with Wallace. We came into parenting with no experience upon which to draw other than knowing a large purple dinosaur loomed large in our future. The honeymoon period of our return home from Russia really ended with the whole giardia adventure. Elisabeth and I are very grateful for the quick diagnosis and treatment, but the whole subject matter was anything other than cute. More importantly, we quickly realized that Wallace needed extra help.

After Wallace's initial pediatric appointment, we had him evaluated for the Early Intervention Program (EIP), which provides services to infants and young children. Our local county department of health and human services describes the EIP as a program "to serve infants and toddlers, birth to three years of age, who have developmental delays. This is a strength-based, family-centered program designed to service children and their families in their natural environments, usually the home."[19]

The EIP program accepted Wallace about six weeks after we brought him home from Russia. I should clarify

19 http://www.co.chautauqua.ny.us/226/Early-Intervention-Program, last checked on February 25, 2017.

that the application process only took a couple of weeks after the New Year's holiday. All the while, Wallace ate like a lumberjack (and that's OK).

Wallace received speech therapy, occupational therapy, and some social skills training. The EIP staff was great and wanted Wallace to succeed. It also helped that he rapidly left behind the issue of malnutrition and also began to understand English. The EIP staff met with us at home or with Wallace alone at his daycare. The occupational therapist especially helped with gross motor skills and learning to walk.

Wallace had apparently not crawled very much while in the orphanage, and his leg muscles appeared quite weak when we brought him home. It was both amusing and odd. As Wallace started walking, he would often just fall down for no apparent reason. His physical therapist, with our permission, took Wallace to be screened by an orthopedic surgeon. The surgeon found nothing wrong with Wallace, and his therapist kept working to strengthen his muscles. Eventually, Wallace stopped his random falling, but I often think of this time as his "fainting goat"[20] period.

Wallace's speech therapist helped him make up ground as well. According to the screening, Wallace was about 30 percent delayed in speech development. It is hard to

---

20 http://animals.howstuffworks.com/mammals/fainting-goat.htm, last checked July 3, 2017.

say how much of this was due to physical issues and how much was related to having to learn English. I would say it does not matter because Wallace really enjoyed his speech therapy and quickly rose to an age-appropriate level for his ability to talk. The trick now is getting Wallace to be quiet.

Wallace received varying levels of services from the EIP program for a couple of years. Wallace's diminutive stature helped us to keep him corralled. Wallace also enjoyed working with the EIP service providers. Between all the food he could eat, all of the individual attention, and not living in an orphanage, Wallace was one happy kid. Elisabeth and I were happy, too.

This was really a fun time for all three of us. Wallace especially liked to sing along with us in the car. My lack of a future as a major recording label artist was never in doubt, but I gamely played along with Elisabeth and Wallace. My version of "Itsy Bitsy Spider" made grown men cry (in agony?). Wallace enjoyed exploring our house, his daycare, and any other place we took him. In hindsight, the ADHD was present, but not the anxiety that is so prevalent with RAD kids. Wallace was unabashedly a happy child.

We were moving merrily along, and then Wallace turned three. Our weekday routine was that Elisabeth went to work early, and I got Wallace ready for the day and took him to daycare. Elisabeth picked him up at the end of the day and spent time with him. Our financial situation did not allow for a stay-at-home parent, but we made the best of our circumstances.

Wallace attended the local daycare facility I mentioned earlier, and his teachers really liked him. This was the first time we learned that teachers needed to make accommodations for Wallace. In the three-year-old group, the staff had to have Wallace nap separately from the other kids or A) he would bother the other kids, and B) no one would nap.

Many of Wallace's behaviors seemed normal to us because we initially did not know the difference between a neurotypical child and an ADHD/RAD child. Our pediatrician actively recommended that Wallace be screened for ADHD. We agreed with the screening. To no one's surprise, Wallace was diagnosed with ADHD. However, we were reluctant to medicate our son who was only three at the time. That reluctance would not last until the end of the year.

Wallace was also transitioning out of the EIP program due to his age. The next step was an evaluation for the special education class of Jamestown's Universal Pre-Kindergarten program (UPK). The first evaluation showed that Wallace was not eligible for the special education UPK program. Elisabeth and I were sort of happy. Wallace was "normal." Actually, Wallace still exhibited some developmental delays, just not delayed enough for the special education

UPK program. At least that was the first impression.

Back at the daycare facility, a new director started. She was a tough cookie. Apparently, some of the staff were having a difficult time managing Wallace. Keep in mind he was only three and very small for his age. We met with the director a couple of times, and she made it clear that Wallace had become a problem. Wallace's teachers had a different point of view and wanted to keep Wallace. The director won that argument.

On a cold Saturday morning in early February, the daycare director called without warning. Elisabeth was visiting her mother, and I was home with Wallace. The conversation went something like this:

"Hi, Tom, this is Joan."

"Hi, Joan. This is a pleasant surprise."

"Not really. I have talked with my supervisors, and we have decided that Wallace should not come back to the daycare facility. Ever."

"What do you mean? He is only three."

"Look, Tom, we just do not have the staff to dedicate to Wallace."

The director offered no suggestions or alternatives, and she quickly ended the telephone call. The daycare facility had abruptly asked Wallace to leave, and Elisabeth and I were livid. Wallace was confused, but we managed to get some emergency daycare from my stepmother and

Elisabeth's godmother. They were saints in snowshoes.

To this day, Elisabeth and I do not know what we could have done differently. Wallace appeared to be a healthy, active three-year-old boy. We were not yet really aware of what it means to be the parent of an ADHD child. It would be years before a neuropsychologist would diagnose Wallace with RAD. This was our first clear experience with someone who did not understand Wallace and could not be charmed by him. What Elisabeth and I knew was that Wallace would need a new daycare provider.

I then called the public school psychologist and pleaded to have Wallace reevaluated. The school psychologist agreed to meet with us again. The day we met with the UPK staff, Elisabeth and I had no babysitter, so we brought Wallace with us. Wallace had a grand time at the meeting. He never sat still for entire meeting even after multiple prompts. I think Wallace poked Elisabeth's face (in a completely loving way) about five times per minute. Wallace personified constant motion. It is hard to really paint a picture of just how chaotic Wallace's behavior was that morning. The school psychologist then *got* the problem and stated that Wallace would not be able to participate in a classroom unless he got some help.[21]

---

21 The tough cookie daycare center director had a valid point about Wallace's behavior. This director, however, showed no empathy to Wallace, Elisabeth, or me.

In short order, Wallace was approved for the special education room in UPK. The school psychologist was also able to get the administration to approve the hiring of a classroom aide just for Wallace. It is very uncommon for a school district to hire a full-time aide for just one student, a three-year-old no less. Wallace needed the help.

Elisabeth and I had by then enrolled Wallace in a daycare program run by the former director of his old daycare (not the lady who removed him). She was very sweet and liked Wallace until partway through the *first day*. This daycare was in the director's house. She had remodeled her garage to make it a nice classroom. The director had let the family dog into the classroom to be part of her curriculum. Wallace promptly pulled the dog's tale, and it bit Wallace. Not hard, just a nip like she would to an overly curious puppy. This daycare provider asked Wallace to not come back after the first day. The director never saw having a dog in a daycare facility as a problem and chose the dog over a child.

Elisabeth was the one who found Wallace's next daycare facility. It's near our house, and we can walk there on nice days. Wallace has been there, on and off, for six years now. These folks accept Wallace for who he is and do not let his ADHD/RAD issues stop them from caring for him. They are both tough and loving at the same time.

The Medical Diagnosis and School Issues Intertwined

UPK started soon thereafter. Wallace's third daycare provider transitioned into his afterschool babysitter. Wallace thrived in UPK and enjoyed his year and a half there. His teacher was simply amazing. Kelly said to us the first day that they would never ask Wallace to leave and that he would be happy. In fact, school officials never asked Wallace to leave, he was very happy, and enjoyed being in a classroom.

During that spring, we visited Wallace's pediatrician, Dr. BT, again. We ended up trusting Dr. BT and started Wallace on the first of many different ADHD medications he would come to take. Treating issues related to brain chemistry and function relies in large part on guesswork during the initial treatment. It would take a while to figure out the right medications and dosages, but we noticed that Wallace was able to slow down and focus more. It was about this time that we added our local pharmacist to our speed dial lists.

Wallace's pediatrician rapidly came to the conclusion that Wallace needed to see a psychiatrist. Elisabeth and I agreed. The problem in scenic Jamestown, New York, is that there are very few pediatric psychiatrists. Our local public mental health clinic had a child psychiatrist on staff, and we made an appointment for Wallace to see him.

Wallace saw this psychiatrist for only a short period of time. However, the psychiatrist told us about the difficulty in diagnosing major psychiatric illnesses in young children. He was comfortable diagnosing the ADHD but said that Wallace was too young for him to precisely diagnose anything else. We would all have to wait a few years for Wallace's brain to grow before the psychiatrist could evaluate Wallace for any issues.

Wallace Conquers Elementary School

Wallace spent a year and a half in the special education UPK class in Jamestown and really bloomed. It was the best decision Elisabeth and I had made thus far in Wallace's short life. His teacher then recommended that Wallace start kindergarten at (barely) age five. He was too bored in UPK at that point. Additionally, Wallace had learned to appropriately participate in a classroom setting.

Elisabeth and I were conflicted. In terms of maturity, Wallace could have used another year of pre-kindergarten. Intellectually, Wallace was bored and getting into mischief. A bored Wallace gets into lots of mischief. We trusted the recommendation of his UPK teacher. In the fall of 2009, Wallace started kindergarten at C. C. Ring Elementary

School.

Elisabeth and I remain conflicted about this decision years later. Wallace was clearly done with UPK but was not the most mature boy for his age. Because Wallace was our first, and only, child, Elisabeth and I could not rely on experience for this decision. I sometimes wonder what would have happened if we had kept Wallace back one year. Wallace was at least excited to start kindergarten.

Wallace was able to participate in kindergarten in a general education room. His teacher recognized Wallace's potential and his issues. She is an experienced and gifted teacher. Kindergarten presented some challenges for Wallace, but his teacher made accommodations and he succeeded. Wallace was very proud at the end of the school year. Elisabeth and I were proud of our son. We felt like our family had overcome the cold removal from that daycare facility.

It was during kindergarten that Wallace started in the Suzuki violin program offered through Jamestown Public Schools, which is based on the methods the renowned Japanese violinist Shinichi Suzuki developed to teach music to young children.[22] Elisabeth and I wanted Wallace to grow up in a musical household. Elisabeth sings and plays piano. I am relegated to singing in the shower, but we wanted Wallace to try something different. For the first

---

22 Sadly, Jamestown Public Schools has discontinued this program.

few Suzuki lessons, the children use a macaroni and cheese box with a paint stirrer taped on as the violin neck. I am no Stradivarius, but I was really proud of my craftsmanship in making Wallace's pseudo-violin.

Wallace was able to demonstrate some proficiency at playing the box/stick combination. His Suzuki teacher then let Wallace move up to a real violin. I never knew that violins came in various sizes until Wallace needed one to fit his little hands and arms. Elisabeth and I then purchased the world's smallest violin. The first thing we taught Wallace was that a violin cannot be used to play indoor tennis.

Wallace took violin lessons for a number of years. I cannot say that this road has been smooth. It was a huge parental challenge for Elisabeth and me to get Wallace to practice after his lessons. As I have said at various times in this book, some days are better than others. Wallace was very proud, however, when he was accepted into the beginning level of the Chautauqua Regional Youth Symphony. When he puts his mind to it, Wallace can play very well. It just takes him longer than a neurotypical child to progress through the lessons.

First and second grades followed similar patterns as kindergarten. Wallace was very fortunate to have two wonderfully talented teachers in those years. Wallace had good days and bad days, but his teachers never gave up. They wanted Wallace to succeed, and he did. Wallace was about grade level in academics despite his profound ADHD.[23]

I would like to report that Wallace is a child prodigy and dynamic athlete. Elisabeth would love it if we could say that Wallace will be the person to finally bring peace to the Middle East. I suppose he still could. Realistically, though, Elisabeth and I must acknowledge that Wallace faces challenges in life that might delay his Nobel Prize.

The teachers and staff at Ring Elementary School liked Wallace. He still had to spend a number of hours in the principal's office receiving extra guidance. For example, one of Wallace's favorite tricks was to go into a bathroom stall, lock the door, and then crawl out the bottom. He thought it was hilarious to lock down the boys room. Elisabeth and I found the humor in his actions but never told Wallace (well, until now).

The lunchroom, and its cacophony of sounds, presented new challenges for Wallace in elementary school. We know now that RAD has an anxiety component. For Wallace, loud, crowded places can bring out anxious behaviors. When you add in the appetite-suppressing ADHD medications, Wallace learned to dread lunchtime.

The staff made some more accommodations for

---

23 The RAD diagnosis did not come until the summer after third grade.

Wallace. The school counselor often let Wallace eat his lunch in her office. His teachers regularly let Wallace eat lunch in the classroom after the lunch period had ended. Everyone pitched in to help Wallace (even when chicken surprise was the entrée du jour). Elisabeth and I will always remember the kindness of the teachers and staff at Ring and Lincoln Elementary Schools.

Again, I look back in hindsight and see that there were signs of anxiety and RAD that Elisabeth and I did not comprehend. Wallace was (and still is) a real ham at home. He loves telling stories and singing along to CDs. Elisabeth and I noticed at school, however, that Wallace as very anxious and reserved during school programs for parents. Wallace also had a tough time making friends. Of course we wish now that we had known more about RAD back then, but it is hard to think of a young boy as having multiple neurological disorders.

By the start of third grade, Wallace was having significant trouble participating in a general education classroom. His third grade teacher liked Wallace but felt confounded with his constant disruptions. Wallace was not happy at all. The principal gently suggested that we request to have Wallace evaluated for a special education room. Elisabeth and I readily agreed. We wanted Wallace to get all of the help he needed. I would have written our request for evaluation using crayons on construction paper until Elisabeth reminded me to type a nice letter with complete sentences.

The Committee for Special Education (CSE) met with us. In about ten minutes, CSE approved Wallace to transfer to a special education room. The CSE concluded that Wallace did not have intellectual problems but behavioral problems. This was an 8-1-1 room: up to eight students, one teacher, and one aide. It meant transferring to another elementary school in Jamestown, but it was worth it.

There was one humorous side benefit to becoming a special education student. Wallace was now eligible for bus service.[24] Elisabeth and I had a good laugh at this option. We could just see the bus aide trying to contain a whole busload of kids just like Wallace. Elisabeth and I politely declined the bus service. I drove Wallace to school in the morning, and Elisabeth picked him up at the end of the day. Elisabeth and I learned to like this quiet time we each had with Wallace.

Wallace started in January of that year, right after the winter break, at Lincoln Elementary School. The spring of 2013 was one of the most enjoyable times for Wallace. His new teacher told Elisabeth and me not to worry— she could handle Wallace. His new teacher was amazing

---

24 Jamestown Public Schools do not provide bus service for general education students in grades one through twelve. Most of the kids walk, or their parents drive.

indeed. Wallace improved daily and was happy for the first time since third grade began. Sadly, the first semester of fourth grade were the toughest days of Wallace's young life.

Elementary School and a Big Detour

And now for a complete non sequitur involving Sir Winston Churchill. In 1941, Sir Winston Churchill visited Harrow School in Great Britain and gave a speech. The British had fought hard and triumphed in the Battle of Britain the year before.

"Never give in—never, never, never, never, in nothing great or small, large or petty, never give in except to convictions of honour and good sense."[25]

Elisabeth and I are trying to raise just one child but, in the toughest of times with Wallace, I always remember Churchill's most famous quote from that speech.

---

25 https://www.winstonchurchill.org/resources/speeches/1941-1945-war-leader/never-give-in-harrow-school, last visited on July 3, 2017.

It Does Get Better

Wallace went through five teachers in the fourth grade. We all came to loathe Wallace's fourth grade year. Here's why:

- His third grade special education teacher was supposed to keep Wallace for the fourth grade. That is called *looping* in the education world. Late in August, another school district hired this teacher.

- Wallace's principal hired a new teacher for the start of school. Though young, this new teacher seemed eager. The first day of school was on a Wednesday. She quit on Friday, two days later. The entire Rankin family started to suffer from whiplash.

- The second week of school started with a long-term substitute. This lasted three weeks until the substitute lost control of the entire classroom of five special needs students. Things were so bad that the principal moved the entire class to a small room that had no windows.

- In mid-October, the principal brought in an experienced general education teacher as a long-term substitute. The principal also convinced a retired special education teacher to help in the classroom. This teaching team knew how to work with special needs children and brought desperately needed stability to the classroom.

- In late November, the new permanent teacher started, and the kids moved back to their regular classroom. The new teacher observed and helped the long-term substitute until winter break started. In January, the permanent teacher took over and finished the school year. Unfortunately, Wallace had fallen behind in his academics with all of the instability from the first part of the year.

At this point, the Wallace's school life and treatment really started to intertwine. At first, Wallace's symptoms seemed difficult but manageable. Things then progressed to unbearable and miserable: *Attack of the Fourth Grader!*

I should mention here that Wallace had been treating with another psychiatrist for a number of years. We changed psychiatrists when Wallace was in the second grade. Wallace's medications changed, and the psychiatrist added new medications to help with Wallace's increasing episodes of anger. The medications definitely helped, but Wallace's sessions with his counselor also helped.

In 2013, Wallace's counselor had to leave work for medical reasons. That was another blow for Wallace. He has a great relationship with his current counselor, but that took some time. The instability at school, coupled with getting to know a new counselor, temporarily took away two of Wallace's anchors in life. Elisabeth and I now realize that we should have had Wallace see his counselor more often.

In June 2013, Wallace was finally diagnosed with RAD in addition to his ADHD. We all knew that the ADHD was only part of the problem. Now, we had a new diagnosis and could start to more effectively help Wallace. That took a while though.

Wallace's psychiatrist also advised us not to let violent episodes get too out of hand. We had to consider hospitalization if Wallace was a danger to himself or others. His psychiatrist was firm on this point.

Autumn 2013, fourth grade, was the most difficult time in Wallace's life. Episodes of anger and violence escalated and occurred with more frequency. Wallace would erupt over simple things like brushing his teeth or playing a wrong note while practicing violin. These episodes happened both at home and at school. Some days were scary, really scary. Elisabeth and I had no training in how to deal with these situations. What do you when your nine-year-old son charges at you with flailing fists? Trial and error eventually came to disengagement where we would ignore the behaviors as long as Wallace and we were safe.

Disengagement, sometimes called "planned ignoring," seems counterintuitive to me. The basic idea is to ignore the behavior. Wallace then has no response and, therefore, cannot use the parent's response to escalate his behavior in turn. If no one pays attention to the temper tantrum, then Wallace eventually stops. Elisabeth and I stay calm and disengaged and the "meltdown" ends soon. This is easy to write but initially was very difficult to practice, and still is.

We now return to the fourth grade. The first few months of fourth grade presented a lesson in instability. By December, Wallace's class had settled in on their fourth teacher. Wallace needed an anchor while in school and, instead, found a carousel of teachers. Never ask the question, "How could things possibly get worse?"

The situation came to a crisis in mid-December. Wallace had a violent episode at school where he attacked his teacher and then the principal. Elisabeth could not immediately leave work, but I could. Neither of us knew how bad things were until I arrived at school. Wallace was in the principal's office and still recovering from being restrained. Sweat covered his face, and he whimpered. Everyone in the school office was upset. I could not reach Elisabeth by phone and had to make one of the toughest decisions ever.

Wallace needed to go to the hospital. We could not keep Wallace safe with his anger and violence coming out almost every day. The staff at school were exasperated and literally bruised. Wallace seemed calm at this point, but I knew another episode could happen at any moment. I told Wallace that I was going to get him some help and then drove him to the emergency room of our local hospital.

At the ER, they took Wallace to a mental health examining room. This room is not a standard hospital room. It had a ten-foot ceiling. The only furniture in the room was a hospital bed. The television was mounted in a metal and plastic cabinet high on the wall. There was a bathroom, but the toilet and sink were a one-unit piece of stainless steel. Think prison toilet but with less elegance. There was no toilet seat, and the room was not all that warm if you know what I mean. The door to the room had a magnetic lock controlled at the nurse's station. In short, there was nothing to throw and very little, if anything, that a person could use to harm himself or others.

I met with the on-call mental health physician's assistant. It was all I could do not to break down, but I explained Wallace's diagnoses and his then-current propensity for violence. The physician's assistant called Wallace's psychiatrist, who recommended admitting Wallace to the pediatric mental health unit of the hospital. I agreed—and felt like throwing up.

I believed that I was a failure as a parent and to Wallace. I felt like I had lost all control in my son's life. I felt absolutely miserable but had to stay positive for Wallace, for he would soon walk into a completely unfamiliar place where Mom and Dad would only be visitors.

The next step was for Wallace to be admitted. The

pediatric mental health unit was in another building almost a mile away from the main hospital. Because Wallace was now a patient, I could not drive him over; an ambulance had to take him. Fortunately, Wallace was excited to ride in the ambulance to Jones Hill, the local name for the other medical campus in Jamestown.

Elisabeth and I had talked at this point. Elisabeth drove directly to the pediatric unit at Jones Hill to meet Wallace while I drove my car from the main campus. Wallace still appeared excited and thought he was on a great adventure. He did not even notice when the security guard frisked him for weapons or contraband. (They search every newly admitted patient, no matter the person's age.)

The pediatric mental health unit is not nearly as scary as you might think. It was definitely institutional, but the staff tried to make things as cheerful as possible. The staff allowed us to bring Wallace's clothes from home. The rules allowed Wallace to wear regular clothes during the day and his own pajamas at night. The staff let us help Wallace with his shower to make sure he actually got clean. The nursing team also allowed Wallace to keep a couple of books to read.

Elisabeth and I met with the unit administrator. We went over the insurance information, of course. The administrator said that most children stay in the mental health unit for three to five days. Wallace ended up staying for a week due to an intervening weekend.

Make no mistake, however: This was a hospital, and we all had to follow the rules. There were set visiting hours. We could see Wallace in only designated rooms. A special room existed for kids having violent meltdowns. This was a safe room with carpeted walls and no furniture. Staff at the nurse's station could monitor the patient in the room through a window. I am happy to report that Wallace never had to use this room.

Once the hospital admitted Wallace to the pediatric mental health unit, Elisabeth and I left to go get his clothes, toiletries (as much as a nine-year-old boy has toiletries), and books. When we were alone in the elevator, I finally lost it. The intellectual side of me knew hospitalization was the right choice. The emotional side of me felt like a failure as a parent for having to hospitalize my son because of his behavior. Emotions were winning at that point.

I composed myself enough to drive home—we were still in separate cars. We collected Wallace's things for the hospital and drove back. The clock read 7:30 p.m. at this point, but it seemed like a small lifetime since I took Wallace from school. We helped Wallace settle into his room and put away his clothes. There was no dresser with pullout drawers, only wall-mounted heavy wooden shelves. Elisabeth helped Wallace take a shower while I did the most constructive activity I could think of at the time:

paced in his room.

Visiting hours ended at 8:00 p.m. It was so hard to leave our son at the hospital. He called us shortly after we got home, and we said good night. Sometime after 10:00 p.m., Elisabeth called the nurses station and got a report on how bedtime went. As I remember the conversation now, Wallace essentially passed out from his nighttime medications and emotional exhaustion. Elisabeth ended up calling every night after Wallace had gone to sleep to get one final report.

Wallace never did really like the hospital. Who does? We all found the separation anxiety to be overwhelming. Wallace called us when he felt upset and we checked in when we each had a spare moment.

Elisabeth and I hardly worked while Wallace was in the hospital. Elisabeth's employer was very understanding. I had a number of court appearances scheduled in family court. I called the chief clerk, who very kindly and adjourned all of my cases. I do remember going to my office on the Saturday that Wallace was still in the hospital and sending case updates to the chief clerk.

Elisabeth and I told our family and a small group of friends about Wallace's hospitalization. A number of people visited Wallace while he was in the hospital. Our priest stopped by as well as Elisabeth's sister and niece. I and a friend met Wallace during lunch time the second day he was at the hospital.

One day, during lunch, Wallace generously shared his bologna sandwich with me. He genuinely wanted me to have his sandwich. However, the last thing I wanted to eat was a bologna sandwich made in a hospital, but I humored Wallace. It tasted as you might expect: institutional white bread and bologna, only with less flavor. The packet of yellow mustard added a culinary flare unmatched in modern sandwich cuisine.

One of the nicest things that happened while Wallace was in the hospital was a visit by our church's choir director. The youth choir was to sing at the service on the Sunday before Christmas, and Wallace had a small solo in the song. Unfortunately, Wallace was not able to leave the hospital to attend church. The choir director came over to the hospital and sang the song with Wallace. He got to sing his solo for Elisabeth and me at least.[26] I think Elisabeth and I will always remember the kindness of the choir director.

Many of our visits with Wallace took place in the pediatric unit's family room. The room did give us some amount of privacy. The lack of TV and other electronics in the room helped us focus on family time. On the other hand, the room's temperature consistently hovered at

26 Wallace finally got to sing this particular solo in church two years later.

about 85 degrees with all the ventilation of a hermetically sealed box. I still think to this day that the hospital charged extra for this sauna service.

In-patient hospitalization really addresses a person's problems on a short-term basis. The purpose of Wallace's hospitalization was to stabilize him and then engage our entire family in further outpatient services. Elisabeth and I agreed to try anything that would potentially help Wallace and us as parents. We enrolled in a program that assigned us a family advocate. This person met with us every week to ten days, and Wallace still has a caseworker that helps us navigate the world of living with a child who has a mental illness.

We also applied to a program to give Wallace more counseling services. Wallace was approved for the highest level of service. He had his own caseworker and met with therapists twice a week. He also now meets with his mental health counselor once per week privately and then in a group session.

One of the most important aspects of Wallace's hospitalization centered on the staff working with Elisabeth and me. We learned that we were not bad parents and to accept Wallace's mental health diagnoses as medical conditions. We learned to encourage Wallace to use his new coping skills. Wallace's psychiatrist only tweaked his medications in a very minor way. And we learned that

Wallace's future mental health would not come in a little brown bottle. Elisabeth and I finally came to understand the role of counseling and therapeutic skill building in Wallace's treatment plan.

If you ask Wallace now, he can name seven to ten coping skills to use when he gets mad or anxious. He learned a few at the hospital and even more with his various counselors and therapists. The trick is convincing Wallace to use his coping skills. With RAD kids, the part of the brain that controls rational conduct becomes strikingly disconnected from the other parts of the brain when the child is angry or upset. One of our long-term goals is helping Wallace keep the rational part of his brain from totally disconnecting when he is upset.

Back to the hospital: Wallace stayed for a week. He hated not being able to sleep at home or being able to see Elisabeth and me outside of visiting hours. We visited every day at least twice per day (braving the presentation of new and improved bologna sandwiches and tropical visiting rooms). We could tell that Wallace seemed calmer, and he certainly wanted to leave. Wallace came home on Christmas Eve, and we all had a lovely Christmas holiday.

Learning to Navigate in Wallace's World

Wallace came home from Russia in December. Eight years later, Wallace came home from the hospital in December. In each situation, our story did not end. Life for everyone, including Wallace, continues after these important life events.

Things have improved since Wallace's stay in the hospital. However, Wallace still struggles with ADHD and RAD. Some days are difficult, and some are better. The flat out violence of late 2013 became sporadic and isolated. Now, these episodes occur primarily in the early morning or early evening.

We have adjusted the timing of Wallace's morning medications, which has greatly reduced the incidence of trouble in the morning. Most trouble now takes place in the very late afternoon or early evening when he is tired, hungry, and his daytime medications have worn off. There are some days with no bad episodes. When there is an episode, it tends to end quickly. Violence is still an issue, but we continue to work with Wallace's team on solutions. More importantly, as he has grown older, Wallace has developed a self-awareness that he did not have in elementary school. Wallace will, on many occasions, seek less violent ways of expressing his anger.

Our social life has changed as well. Noisy, crowded places challenge Wallace, so we avoid putting Wallace in those settings. That means attending fewer family parties, especially in the evening. Going out to eat more likely happens now for breakfast or lunch and not very often for dinner. Elisabeth and I give ourselves permission to leave early if Wallace is having a tough time. We do not view this as punishment but rather taking Wallace out of an environment that causes him (and us) to feel miserable.

Some days, it seems like we are isolating Wallace, and ourselves, from the rest of society. This may be true to a certain extent. Wallace often struggles in new environments, especially those in which there is no accommodation for his special needs. Elisabeth and I are very careful now not to place Wallace in settings that are likely to be too challenging. We all accept that there are many instances in this world where Wallace will have to conform if he is to lead any semblance of a normal life. Elisabeth and I now see our primary jobs as preparing Wallace for adulthood knowing that he is not (yet) neurotypical.

We also celebrate things that seem odd to some. Wallace has a very difficult time with peer relations. Elisabeth and I cheer loudly when he shows good sportsmanship to other kids. Successful violin concerts mean a rare evening trip to Friendly's for ice cream. Completing math homework usually earns a big hug and strong praise. A small thing to a neurotypical child can be a big thing for Wallace. We celebrate the good times no matter how mundane.

Wallace's elementary school experience was far from typical. Wallace faced new challenges, including hair gel and girls, in middle school. Elisabeth and I feel happy to have made it through elementary school.

To Middle School and Beyond!

The end of fourth grade brought a major milestone in Wallace's life. Wallace successfully completed not only fourth grade but elementary school as well. On a humid rainy morning in late June, all of the fourth grade parents (and grandparents) filed into the delightfully *not* air-conditioned auditorium at Lincoln Elementary School. You could feel the excitement and perspiration in the air.

Apparently, the children were under very strict orders not to do anything crazy. As the principal read each name, the child in question marched up to the podium as if on a solemn march. Wallace was one of the last kids to be called. He was dressed in his white shirt, bow tie, and black pants. This was one of the proudest moments of his life, and we were very happy for Wallace.

Just six months earlier, Wallace was having a very difficult time resulting in a hospital stay. The principal straddled the fence as to Wallace's return to school. The alternative would have been a school for children extreme mental health issues or juvenile delinquency problems. Wallace, to his great credit, worked hard to stabilize and finished the school year.

Unfortunately, elementary school graduation may have

been the high point of Wallace's summer.

The summer after fourth grade was fraught with too many things. Wallace's anxiety and inability to remain consistently calm all day prevented us from sending Wallace to a traditional overnight camp. This was disappointing to Elisabeth and me because there are a number of wonderful summer camp programs located on Chautauqua Lake.

Elisabeth's own activity skyrocketed. He employer is our local state assemblyman, and it was an election year. This meant collecting ballot signatures early in the summer. Wait! There's More! Our (very) local county legislature seat became open, and Elisabeth decided to run in the special election to fill the position. That meant even more ballot signatures and then campaigning.

Back to Wallace: We knew from years of experience that Wallace did well in certain types of summer day camps and not so well in other day camp programs. (Wallace does best in small, less institutionalize programs.) And while there are many wonderful summer day camps in our area, the one drawback is that these camps last only a week at a time. That meant Wallace went from camp to camp throughout the summer.

For the most part, Wallace enjoyed his camp experiences. The Audubon camp gave Wallace the chance to spend lots of time outdoors and then spend time writing in a journal. The Audubon staff knows Wallace and was very understanding when he needed to take a break from class. One morning, he took a one-hour nap in the director's office and then returned to the program. Nobody became anxious, and Wallace seemed much happier after his nap.

Other camps included a half-day basketball camp, soccer camp, cultural exploration camp, two different vacation Bible schools, and a unique day camp at the Children's Safety Education Village[27]. Each of these camps was really great for Wallace. The only problem was changing camps from week to week. Elisabeth and I spent a lot of time with Wallace to help him prepare for the weekly changes in camps.

Wallace also spent time this summer becoming more independent on his bicycle. We live in a quiet neighborhood where the most serious crime occurs when someone forgets to put out their weekly recycling bin. Wallace spent many hours riding around our neighborhood. As it turns out, Wallace also went beyond our established geographic boundaries and suffered significant time without his bike

27 "The Children's Safety Education Village is a Not-For-Profit Organization that caters to preventing unnecessary injuries and unfortunate fatalities of children in our community through education and first-hand experience." http://www. childrenssafetyvillage.com/, last visited on April 1, 2016.

as a consequence.[28]

Wallace also struggled with his mental health. His physical aggression at home escalated, becoming more frequent and more violent. Several months earlier, Wallace decided that Elisabeth was "dirty" and did not want any physical affection from her. It is hard to describe what it is like to be absolutely rejected by your child. This was just devastating to Elisabeth. Because of Wallace's behavior on Mother's Day morning, Elisabeth ate breakfast alone at Friendly's while I dealt with Wallace. Heartbreaking.

Another issue that became more pronounced was waking up in the morning. We came to learn that Wallace is not a morning person—at all. Wallace redefines the word grouchy when he wakes up. Many mornings in the summer, Wallace woke up and started hitting and kicking us even after we had adjusted his morning routine to help us all. This presented a very challenging time for Elisabeth and me. We soon figured out a system: Wallace would take his morning pills and, in return, we would then leave him alone for about ten minutes. Getting up and getting dressed remained unpleasant, but the morning medications would eventually take control and calm down Wallace.

When things really got out of hand, we took Wallace to

---

28 Wallace felt quite certain that we would not mind if he drove to the 7-Eleven over a mile away at the corner of two busy streets. To quote Jim Carrey as the Grinch, "Wrong-o!"

our local hospital. At the emergency room, Wallace would then stabilize because he wanted to avoid readmission to the mental health unit. As Wallace's psychiatrist re-explained at one point, hospitalization exists really to stabilize the child and engage him/her in necessary services. Wallace was already engaged in mental health services, and his psychiatrist wanted us to ride out the periodic episodes of violence. In other words, Wallace did not really need overnight hospitalization due to his level of treatment and services. The intellectual side of us understood Wallace's psychiatrist. The emotional side of us felt exhausted.

On top of the mental health issues, Wallace intently experienced life to its fullest. That meant the following for the summer of 2014: a $2 skateboard followed by one sprained ankle, one squirrel bite, three or four frogs captured and released, purple hair, about half a dozen pairs of socks who made the ultimate sacrifice, a tree climbing event that required a trip to the emergency room, and a bout of severe constipation requiring a special prescription from the doctor and an IV in the emergency room.

Stability was not a word we used very often during this summer after fourth grade. One thing Elisabeth and I managed to do during summer was to regularly discuss with Wallace the transition to Washington Middle School. In Jamestown, middle school encompasses fifth through eighth grades. We often drove to the middle school during the summer to get Wallace acclimated to going there. At one point in August, Wallace got to go visit his teacher while she was setting up her classroom. As much as we prepared Wallace, he was still very anxious on the first day of school.

The morning of the first day of fifth grade was quite unpleasant. Wallace woke up hitting and swearing like a sailor. Elisabeth tried to spend a few minutes talking with him on our front porch. Wallace reacted with more foul language and hitting. He then moved on to me. But we eventually got him to school, and he had a good day.

After school, Wallace again attacked Elisabeth. It was as if Wallace used all his skills to have good behavior in school but then lost control once the school day ended. Wallace was still agitated when I got home from work and attacked me. Elisabeth and I then took Wallace to the hospital. Three attacks in one day was too much. If Wallace was truly having a breakdown, then he needed to be in a safe environment.

Wallace calmed down and stabilized at the hospital. The hospital staff dispensed his nighttime medications. About an hour later, Wallace was groggy and ready to go home. It might seem strange that we felt Wallace needed to go to the hospital to calm down. After the third attack, however, Elisabeth and I really did not know what was going to happen next. When I say attack, I mean real fists and feet of fury.

Wallace's anxiety level slowly decreased over the next week. He was doing fine in school but not terribly well at home. Wallace still rejected Elisabeth for the most part. At least he was not attacking us every day, just several times per week.

At this point in time, Wallace was taking many medications. The morning started with four different ones. The medications, in theory, focused on Wallace's ADHD, anxiety, and anger issues. Adderall was one of these medications. I mention this because Wallace's therapist soon advocated that Wallace stop taking it.

At lunchtime, Wallace would take an Adderall booster at school. Around 3 p.m., Wallace would take boosters of two different medications he took in the morning. Wallace took a final dose of medications to help him sleep around 8 p.m. I want to be clear that Wallace was not taking traditional sleeping pills but different doses of two of his morning medications.

Wallace had a terrible time falling asleep prior to taking the nighttime medication. He would sometimes be awake, and active, after 11 p.m. Wallace was miserable as were Elisabeth and I (and the dog for that matter). However, these particular medications were a real blessing and allowed Wallace to get back to a normal sleep schedule.

However, it remained that Wallace was taking daily four

different medications in fairly high daily doses. Wallace's psychiatrist also prescribed a fifth medication to help Wallace calm down when very agitated. The trick with this fifth medication was to give it to Wallace before things got out of hand. This timing issue frustrated us because Wallace could escalate too quickly. Let me put it another way: Wallace usually did not give us a thirty-minute warning prior to having a violent, angry meltdown.

The 3 p.m. medication also had a side effect of increasing Wallace's appetite. There were quite a few evenings when Wallace was just frantic with hunger.

In late September, we switched therapists after finding one who specializes in RAD. Wallace's new therapist, Mary[29], told Elisabeth and me that Wallace had a very pronounced case of RAD. Mary consulted with a psychologist (not in our immediate area) about Wallace. They recommended that Wallace stop taking the Adderall because the Adderall might be increasing Wallace's overall level of anger.

Elisabeth and I consulted with Wallace's treating psychiatrist, who was not eager to switch Wallace to a new ADHD medication. But Wallace's psychiatrist did recommend a new medication to address Wallace's anger and anxiety. This new medication replaced two of

---

29 This is not her real name. If she gives me permission, I will use her real name in a future edition of this book.

Wallace's other medications. We tried the new medication, and Wallace seemed to not tolerate it. We ended up in the emergency room one night, and the medical staff had us go back to the other two medications.

About ten days later, Wallace had a regularly scheduled appointment with his psychiatrist. The doctor wanted us to try again with the new medication. Elisabeth and I had talked already about this recommendation. We wanted Wallace to try the new medication but in a controlled environment. Wallace's psychiatrist agreed, and we admitted Wallace to the pediatric mental health unit at our local hospital.

Wallace was very unhappy. He was both angry and sad.

"I promise that I will never hit or kick again! I promise!"

"You have said that many times before, Wallace," I said evenly. "You cannot hit people when you are mad."

"I'll try. I'll really try this time!" exclaimed Wallace.

"Wallace, going to the hospital is not a punishment. The hospital is a place for you to get help and be safe at the same time."

"I'll be safe. I will!"

The biggest problem, from Wallace's perspective, was being separated from Mom and Dad while at the hospital. Elisabeth and I did not feel we could keep Wallace (and us) safe should he have an adverse reaction to any new medications. At the same time, we felt horrible having to place Wallace in the hospital.

Wallace threw a fit when we arrived at the hospital. His psychiatrist told us to report to the emergency department, where the admission would take place.

"I won't go! I won't go!"

The reception clerk put on Wallace a plastic wristband with all of Wallace's pertinent information. Wallace then ripped it off. I managed to guide Wallace to the waiting area.

"I won't go!" yelled Wallace as he made a break for the front door.

I managed to block Wallace's path, and he hit me a few times. However, I used this deflection to guide Wallace away from the front door. Elisabeth and I sat with Wallace and held him, but he struggled.

"Honey, you need to be safe. We love you and want you to come home right away, but you cannot act like this."

(A few inappropriate, salty words from Wallace.)

This went on for a number of minutes, and then a nurse's assistant came out. Frank was very kind and gentle with Wallace. Frank was also well over six feet tall and could easily carry Wallace and the couch on which he was sitting.

"Hi, Wallace. I'm Frank. Why don't you take my hand and come with me."

Wallace had to crane his neck to see Frank's face. There

was a pause while Wallace contemplated the situation. Wallace apparently decided that Frank meant business.

"OK," said Wallace, and he took Frank's hand.

Wallace did not give us any more trouble that day. He cried and was generally unhappy, but the violence stopped. Frank never raised his voice and was always kind to Wallace. I think Wallace finally realized that fighting us would not lead to going home.

Within hours of his admission, we knew we had made the right choice. Wallace's psychiatrist saw Wallace in the late afternoon, about two hours after admission. He was surprised at Wallace's level of anger and immediately recommended that Wallace discontinue the Adderall and start a non-stimulant ADHD medication as well as the new anxiety medication contemplated a few weeks ago. Elisabeth and I readily agreed.

Wallace spent five and a half days in the hospital. He showed no adverse reaction to the new medications and had time to adjust to them before going home. Compared to his first hospitalization, Wallace was very weepy this time. He would call Elisabeth and me at night terribly upset and would beg us to take him home. These were the worst phone calls.

"Mommy, Iamsorry Iwanttocomehome!" wept Wallace into the telephone.

"We love you, Wallace. You are getting better every

day," answered Elisabeth.

"Please, Mommy, please!"

"Sweetheart, Dad and I will come see you again tomorrow. You need to get some rest now; it's late."

"Please Mommy, please!"

"Dad and I are never far away. If you keep improving, you will come home in a couple of days. So try to sleep. Things will be better in the morning."

"All right," sniffled Wallace.

"We love you bigger than the sky."

"I love you so much."

"Will you try to sleep now?"

"All right. Good night, Mom."

"Good night, sweetie."

Elisabeth and I visited every day. We actually had some good family time. Wallace was always happy to see us. He started sitting in Elisabeth's lap again. A couple of times, he fell asleep in Elisabeth's arms. Wallace, after many months of frostiness, crossed the divide that separated him from Elisabeth. Mom was back. Elisabeth looked and sounded so much better after Wallace started accepting her again. I think this accelerated Wallace's recovery. Elisabeth relished her newly returned relationship with Wallace.

Wallace also demonstrated some new coping skills. Wallace learned, in theory, to accept a compliment. Some other coping skills included takin a self-initiated time out, asking for help, and going on a walk. It became clear to the medical staff and us, as parents, on day five that Wallace was ready to come home.

We all enjoyed Wallace's homecoming. He was so happy and excited the first night that he was home. Wallace's excitement kept him up late but in a positive way. But there was one problem: Wallace left the hospital on the same day as the monster snowstorm hit Buffalo. This was the storm that left five to seven feet of snow in places. Our local pharmacy did not have the new ADHD medication in stock and had to order it. Unfortunately, the snowstorm interrupted their medication delivery for a few days.

Old Man Winter was no match for Angry Elisabeth protecting her son. Elisabeth had suffered many months of alienation from Wallace. In no way would Elisabeth now let a once-in-a-century storm stop Wallace from getting his medication. I pity the people who tried to deter Elisabeth during that week.

Elisabeth the Lioness sprang into action calling medical providers all over town in search of samples. Most agencies said something like, "You want what? No, we don't have that medication." It was at that point that Elisabeth seethed with anger and frustration. Her ears vented steam.

Finally, one of the local agencies did have some samples, and fortunately, Wallace's psychiatrist was affiliated with this agency. Elisabeth obtained a week's supply of the new ADHD medication, and Wallace missed his dose by only twelve hours. Our pharmacy's supply of the new medication arrived a few days later. Elisabeth wanted to personally escort the UPS delivery person to our pharmacy and offered to provide a water cannon salute as it approached the delivery entrance.

Life settled into the new normal after that. Wallace continued to either seek, or at least accept, Elisabeth's affection. Things became a little tense between Wallace and me as he adjusted to spending more time with Elisabeth. Wallace was much more active and fidgety as compared when he was taking Adderall. We all willingly accepted this as the cost of getting rid of Adderall's propensity to make Wallace angry all of his waking hours.

Elisabeth and I thought that Wallace should have calmed down at school after his discharge from the hospital. Unfortunately, Wallace's behavior at school took a turn for the worse. His teacher communicated with us on a daily basis, and it was quite apparent that Wallace had regressed with his behavior. School presented a problem for Elisabeth and me. We did not observe the behavior, and we did not want to re-punish Wallace at home if his teacher had already addressed an issue. Elisabeth and I did our best to support Wallace and his teacher.

Things came to a semi-crisis a couple of weeks after Wallace had returned home from the hospital. The new

ADHD medication only partially addressed Wallace's fidgety behavior. Wallace was also not sleeping well. Elisabeth and I wrote a letter to Wallace's psychiatrist and detailed our observations of Wallace since leaving the hospital. We also asked for an increase in the dosage of the ADHD medications and, reluctantly, a reintroduction of one of the medications discontinued in the hospital.

Within twenty-four hours of sending this letter to the staff at Wallace's psychiatrist's office, they called us with a new appointment. The new appointment was only two days later.[30] Wallace's psychiatrist stated that an incremental change in the ADHD medicine would not do much for Wallace. He recommended trying a much larger dose, and we agreed. Wallace's psychiatrist also agreed to the reintroduction of one of the old medicines at night to help with sleeping.

As I close this part of the chapter, all of us are hoping the new medication scheme helps Wallace. Our little guy deserves to have a nice life.

On the therapy front, the new therapist is very knowledgeable about RAD. The basic idea is to make Wallace's world small and treat him like he was two or three. This is not regression therapy but rather taking time to give Wallace a chance to bond with us in a way he could

---

30 There are times when we have to wait a month for an appointment. Parents are the best advocates for their children.

not while living in the orphanage.

Making Wallace's world small required a big gulp from Elisabeth and me. We took Wallace out of group violin classes, piano classes, and team sports. Wallace spends a lot more time with us, which was one of the goals of his therapist. Aside from school, Wallace must spend all of his time with either Elisabeth, me, or the both of us. Work requirements sometimes interfere and Wallace goes to his babysitter, but this occurs only on exceptionally busy days.

We should still do more. Ideally, Elisabeth would take a six-month sabbatical and homeschool Wallace. Our finances just do not allow such a move right now. We would do this in a heartbeat if we could afford it. Our local school is not the issue. Homeschooling would allow ample opportunity for parent-child bonding. Wallace deserves the chance to have the exclusive time with parents that infants normally get and need.

We Cannot Wait for Puberty to Find Wallace

Wallace is still a child but will be a teenager sooner than we want. Wallace's life challenges will continue and change over time. Elisabeth and I want Wallace to have every opportunity to succeed in life. This means we must adapt as Wallace grows older and his body changes.

We also want Wallace to accept his challenges without

feeling as if he must hide them. Wallace's time in the hospital was probably the least fun all three of us ever had. However, Wallace's stays in the hospital put him on a clearer path to mental health. Wallace should not feel ashamed of having spent time in the hospital. Elisabeth and I are grateful that Wallace has improved greatly since his stays there. We acknowledge this in the same way a person might celebrate improved health after a course of chemotherapy. No one has ever described chemotherapy as enjoyable, but people who survive cancer are grateful for a renewed chance at life.

People with mental illnesses, especially children, should not be shunned but embraced.

Wallace and Sensory Issues

While Wallace may have significant mental health and behavioral issues, the neurological aspect of his issues often come out in the form of sensory exploration. A piece of toast to Wallace is not just food but a thing to explore with hands, eyes, and nose as well. Wallace touches all of his food, even clearly hot soup.

This makes teaching proper table manners an interesting challenge. Wallace knows how to set the table and fold napkins. As soon as we sit down, however, he looks at everything as a giant finger bowl.

Food texture also trumps taste. Wallace spent an entire year refusing to eat mashed potatoes because of texture. Most kids look at mashed potatoes as both a building material and the best thing to eat. Wallace looked at mashed potatoes as just shy of evil.

An edible product of Mother Nature also causes Wallace to test his senses. Jamestown receives on average about ninety-seven inches of snow per year.[31] Wallace likes to put his hand in every inch of new snow and taste it. This exploration involves both touch and taste. The cleanliness of the snow is never an issue for Wallace, but Elisabeth and I do steer him away from any yellow snow. Wallace's exploration of snow started when he learned to walk and continues today. When I take Wallace sledding in the winter, he takes forever walking back up the hill because he must stop every three feet to taste the snow.

Blankets are another important part of Wallace's life. He often needs to have a blanket on him at bedtime, TV time, and meal times if we let him. Bedtime seems obvious, but Wallace wants a blanket even on the warmest of evenings. He then asks Elisabeth or me to tuck the blanket under his mattress.

"Mom, will you please tuck me in?" asked Wallace.

"Sure, honey, but you do not need all these blankets."

"Yes, I do. And the blue one goes first and then my *Star Wars* blanket."

Whereupon Wallace proceeds to direct Elisabeth in the Layering of the Blankets ritual.

---

31 Albany, Binghamton, Buffalo, Rochester, and Syracuse all compete for the Golden Snowball every year. The winner is the city with the most snowfall during the winter season, http://www.goldensnowball.com. I think Jamestown could easily win this contest on any given year

This is fine with us but again highlights Wallace's need for a sensory input that goes beyond what you might normally expect. Additionally, it was about 70 degrees in Wallace's room. The danger of hypothermia did not seem apparent to us. Wallace, however, focused more on the cocoon-like feeling that all the blankets combined to make.

Smell is also important to Wallace. He has discovered my cologne and Elisabeth's perfume. I also have an ancient bottle of Old Spice that I have never thrown away due to inertia. It is now common for Wallace, and the entire upstairs, to reek of Old Spice. He is the manliest sixth grader in town. Part of this is experimentation, but Wallace clearly seeks out certain smells to keep around him.

"OK, Wallace, time to go!" I might sometimes bark when we're headed out.

"Just a minute! I need my cologne!" replies the best-smelling kid on our block.

Wallace then took his personal bottle of spray and doused himself in a haze of weird-smelling stuff.

"Dad, I smell good and manly!"

"You certainly smell like a junior high school kid."

Recently, Wallace and I ventured out on the evening of Black Friday, the day after Thanksgiving. We stopped by our local mall to grab a sandwich at Wallace's favorite nationally franchised submarine sandwich place. After our dining on handcrafted sandwiches, Wallace insisted on going to the mall's smelly soap store. We stepped into the store with all of its smells, and Wallace visibly relaxed. He took me by the hand to his favorite sample bottles. I should point out that we were the only males in the store, but Wallace did not let that slow down his march to smell every bottle possible.

Wallace had become enamored with the scent of lavender at this point in his life. Fearless, my eleven-year-old son approached an employee for directions to the lavender section of the store. I learned that evening that this store really had a lavender section. The number of lavender products certainly surprised me but not Wallace. I did consent to buying Wallace some lavender-scented shower gel. Wallace spent the rest of the evening extoling the virtues of lavender.

As this book goes to press, Wallace has some of the best-maintained hair in Jamestown. Why? Wallace has learned that Mom's conditioner smells good. It is common now for Wallace to try each shampoo and conditioner he can find during bath time. There is no real harm in this olfactory exploration, but it brings about a most unusual demand: "Dad, smell my hair!"

This reminds of the time a few years ago when Wallace and I were left to ourselves while Elisabeth went to visit her brother in eastern Pennsylvania.

The Hand Lotion That Ate Jamestown

The Monday after the Super Bowl often means waking up early after a long night of wings, beer, and Spam. When Elisabeth was visiting her out-of-town brother, the stage was set for a little pandemonium with young Master Wallace. I prefer to call it Sleepless on Arlington Avenue, but that is another story. This little episode took place when Wallace was five or six.

Wallace usually woke up around 7:20 to 7:30 in the morning, just after I finished my shower and donned my gray flannel uniform, er, suit for the day. This particular Monday was Super-Letdown Monday, the day after Phoenix lost to Pittsburgh in Super Bowl 43.[32] Wallace arose early that morning at 6:45, loudly announcing his presence by calling out, "Daddy! Hello!" Wallace looked awfully cute in his *Cars* pajamas. Soon, however, the junior cowboy/spaceman would battle a very smelly foe.

Springing to life, I greeted Wallace at the threshold to the master suite. Our dog, Chip, and I had been conducting a postgame analysis on the Cardinals' heartbreaking loss to the Steelers when Wallace decided that he wanted to expound on the virtues of Handy Manny, a cartoon philosopher employed by the Disney Channel.

---

32 I am Roman numeral impaired.

I dutifully installed Wallace on the Big Bed and put on the aforementioned Handy Manny, hoping that Wallace would take the hint and fix our leaky basement. With a stern warning about leaving the comfy confines of the Big Bed, I left Wallace to contemplate Handy Manny's crisis du jour while I began my morning shower.

Ahhh, The Hot Shower of Happiness. Nothing could interfere with my twenty minutes of nirvana.

The door then burst open. "Dad! Chippy is growling at me!" The cold hallway air gripped my ankles. Wallace frequently forgot that Chip's tail was *not* a baton for conducting music. (This was also when Wallace regularly watched *Little Einsteins*.)

"OK, OK. Chip! Come here. Good boy." I sent Wallace back to Not-So-Handy Manny and invited Chip into the inner sanctum (i.e., bathroom) to express his views on Kurt Warner's throwing arm. Calm was briefly restored.

The door burst open again. "Dad, smell my hands!"

"Huh? Get back on the Big Bed!"

Something *had* caused Wallace's hands to smell funny, but I had failed to grasp the situation. Now, a more alert father would have instantly grasped the emergency and acted right away.

Not me.

I was under the influence of Suave Shampoo and did not register the danger signal.

All good showers must come to an end. I was calmly drying my feet when another blast of arctic hallway air slammed into me.

"Dad, SMELL MY HANDS!" This expression should scare any parent, but I could only muster a mildly coherent response."

"Huh?"

Then, I glanced at two small hands drenched in Elisabeth's hand lotion. *Drenched.* It was as if Wallace had mixed up a bowl of the odious lavender goo by hand while boldly flouting the child labor laws of the state of New York. I also noticed the runoff on Wallace's favorite *Cars* pajamas.

I sprang into action as only a forty-two-year-old dad wearing nothing but a bath towel can do. I guided the junior mad scientist by his shoulder and instructed him in no uncertain terms to sit on the toilet while I finished drying my not quite middle-aged torso. Chip went to a neutral corner and watched the action unfold.

All this lasted about thirty seconds until Wallace decided to parade around the increasingly crowded bathroom. He seemed interested in the subtleties of leading a marching band. I again seized control of the situation and placed Wallace on the bathroom counter with pointed instructions to now remain sitting until he was twenty-seven.

Finally adorned in boxer shorts and a terribly white T-shirt, I began the decontamination process. We still had some pre-moistened wipes around, which I quickly acquisitioned for the battle. A large pile of used wipes and a few choice "Daddy words" later, the first finger was clean. I then managed to get Wallace's hands, wrists, and forearms clean with an added bonus of expanding the young boy's foreign word vocabulary. Times like this make me proud that I can curse in German, Spanish, French, Russian, and Japanese.

I then seized the moment and had Wallace try to dress himself while still in a temporary state of cleanliness. As Wallace attempted to put his socks on his elbows, I quickly ran into the master suite to survey the damage. Thankfully, the carnage was limited to the TV stand. Water may never again penetrate the lotioned area, but I was able to clean up the area without the assistance of the Environmental Protection Agency. Elisabeth's bottle of lotion, however, had made the ultimate sacrifice.

Here now was the situation: one child who thought his socks should cover his forearms, one newly waterproofed TV stand, and one father setting a fine example for balding men across the nation. At least the dog and cat (Lulu) enjoyed the show.

Luckily, Elisabeth had ironed a clean shirt for me. L.L. Bean called the fabric "luxuriously thick." I called it a tarp with a button-down collar. After dressing, I explained to Wallace the purpose of foot hosiery and helped him put his socks on the correct limbs. Wallace and I even managed to find matching socks that he most likely had not worn yet this week.

Sadly, Jamestown Public Schools had declared Super Bowl Monday to be a "teacher in-service" day, giving the youth of Jamestown a day off from their studies. The timing of the Super Bowl and the in-service day seemed rather curious. Anyway, Wallace and I donned our woolen spacesuits and stepped into the *brisk* winter air. Wallace and I then alighted to his babysitter, where I deposited one child with very supple hands.

I spent the remainder of the day trying to explain to my clients that assaulting your neighbor with a snow shovel is not the best way to resolve boundary disputes, even if the snow shovel is made from plastic and not metal.

It's funny now, and it was funny at the time (if also a bit harrowing), but this episode shows how Wallace's sensory exploration comes up at the most surprising times. To every extent possible, Elisabeth and I let Wallace explore his world. I just hope this exploration does not involve any more pre-dawn lotion testing.

(To this day, our TV stand repels all liquids. Our dog, Chip, is elderly now, but he still pines for the "glory days" of the Arizona Cardinals.)

Raising a Special Needs Child in Church

This chapter is really where this book began. I wanted to share with our church family what it is like to raise a special needs child in the church. The majority of this chapter originally appeared in newsletters put out by the Episcopal Diocese of Western New York.

As you might now imagine, attending church with Wallace brings its own challenges and rewards. (I will just skip over the time Wallace stood up on the pew and yelled, "Geronimo!" in the middle of the service. Yes, he jumped.)

Like many parents, our desire to give our son a religious foundation in life brought us back to regular church attendance. We attend Saint Luke's Episcopal Church in Jamestown. From the first day, the congregation at Saint Luke's has welcomed us, and especially Wallace, into the parish. Of course, Wallace is a force to be reckoned with even in church.

The Rankin family usually sits on the left side of the church so that we can make a quick exit if necessary. Believe me, we have made many quick exits over the years. Trips to the potty and the occasional temper tantrum have caused us to run to the exit. Many families sit on this side of the church for similar reasons.

One of these most famous (or infamous) events started in one of those aforementioned pews on the left side of church. Wallace was about three and had finally mastered the art of running after leaving the fainting goat stage of his life. One Sunday, during the offertory, Wallace managed a jailbreak and took off running right in the middle of the offertory hymn. He went up to the front and over to the center aisle. Elisabeth gave up the chase at that point. I had run to the back of the church and over to the center aisle.

There came Wallace, having a grand time, sprinting down the center aisle much to the delight of the congregation. Fortunately, the ushers were gathered to bring up the collection plates. Wallace tried to run through the khaki forest but ended up slowing down long enough for me to scoop him up. Members of the congregation were openly laughing at this point.

Wallace and I proceeded to return to our pew. Elisabeth and I wanted to move to North Dakota at this point. Wallace, however, was full of joy. He said, "Daddy, I ran really fast!" I looked at his beaming face and said, "Yes, you did, Son!" We hugged and sat down with Elisabeth. After church, we were waiting to be scolded, but the opposite occurred. Many people approached us to say that they enjoyed Wallace's jailbreak and how we responded.

Then there was the time our former rector planted a seed that caused some commotion. Elisabeth and I had decided to attend the Saturday evening service and took Wallace with us. He was still about three or four. We arrived early and were chatting with our former rector in the main church. Father Eric decided it would be cool to teach Wallace to yell, "Echo!" in the church. Wallace thought this was a great idea when we took our seats in the smaller chapel.

Tragically, Wallace did not know when to stop. At various points in the Saturday service, Wallace would yell out, "Echo!" Elisabeth and I were ready to enroll in the Episcopal Witness Protection Program. I think it is based in northern North Dakota. We managed to get through the service with only a few odd looks from other parishioners. Wallace had the best time ever.

Our former rector had two young girls. As Elisabeth and I pondered the spiritual ramifications of payback, we vowed to get each of his girls their own drum sets. Father Eric still laughs when I remind him of this story.

Our former rectors and current rector have been wonderful with Wallace. They can see God's work in this little boy. Sometimes Wallace has some fairly profound theological questions such as "How do families find each other in Heaven?" or "Mom, how did Hell actually start?" "Which came first, time or God? These are the questions that stump Elisabeth and me as parents. Thankfully, Saint Luke's interim rector and new rector each have had an open door for Wallace and help him with these important religious questions.

One of Wallace's favorite activities is helping me when I usher. Wallace has learned how to count (with occasional accuracy) the number of people who come to church, to help pass the offering plate, and is a great greeter. On the other hand, having Wallace as a junior usher has created the need for some never-before-needed rules:

- Ushers do not butt dance in church.
- Ushers do not eat all of the cookies at coffee hour.
- Ushers do not contemplate shooting misbehaving people with paintball guns.
- Ushers do not play in the parking lot *during* church.
- Ushers do not fill out pew cards in the name of "Seymour Butts."

These new rules have helped clarify Wallace's role as a junior usher.

The Saint Luke's community is very understanding and supportive of Wallace. He has dropped the collection plate only once. More importantly, the people of Saint Luke's want Wallace to succeed in life and can see he is trying. I often think God takes Wallace's hand as he goes through his day.

As I wrote in a Facebook post, Wallace had a particularly

eventful Palm Sunday in 2014:

Wallace Enters Jerusalem

Today, Palm Sunday, was the nicest weather day of the year so far. We were in the 60s this morning. For the first time in years, Saint Luke's was able to have the Palm Sunday processional outside. Wallace and I participated, creating an unplanned liturgy, so to speak. During the first part of the processional, Wallace struck up a conversation with our interim priest where he explained his various wounds. Wallace had a scooter wreck yesterday and was eager to explain all of his bumps and scrapes. The Palm Sunday processional was a perfect time to get the clergy's attention—nothing else was going on (at least in the mind of one nine-year-old). Explaining the Great Scooter Crash of 2014 took Wallace's attention away from holding stuff. Wallace then dropped his book (*Captain Underpants*) whereupon he uttered quite loudly, in the Palm Sunday processional, "Oh Crap!" This delighted those around us but created more gray hairs on Dad. (We safely recovered the slightly scratched book.) When we got to the next corner, Wallace said, "Dad, I'm going to 7-Eleven now. See you later." I replied in the only way possible, "Wrongo bongo; stay with me." I then gently guided a disappointed Wallace back into the processional group. We finally reached the front entrance of the church with some very confused ushers. Apparently, no one informed the ushers about our long processional, and they were out in the street looking for us.

And how can I forget this little chestnut:

I'll Be Here All Week

Ahhh, ushering in church on a lovely spring morning. What could go wrong?

- The children's choir had dress rehearsal as the early arrivers started, well, arriving. That was when Wallace grabbed the microphone and impressed us with his extensive repertoire of flatulence noises. The sound system at Saint Luke's is quite good, and I am sure that the YWCA residents across the street were able to here Wallace and his stand-up act.

- Apparently, it was Clergy Bring Your Dog to Church Day. Theo the dog is usually one of our quiet parishioners, but today, Theo did not like the looks of one particular gentleman. During the Old Testament reading, Theo started barking at this person. A fellow usher and I tried to distract Theo but to no avail. The reading pertained to Ezekiel and "dry bones," a favorite passage for dogs according to the lay reader. I think that was the first time I had ever heard a canine commentary on the Old Testament. Our interim priest eventually came down from the altar area and banished Theo to somewhere east of Eden. Theo certainly provided five minutes of comic relief.

- The children's choir performed their song without any improvisation on the part of Wallace. (He thought about it, though.) During the sermon, however, Wallace managed to give himself a paper cut. I took Wallace into the most sacred room in the church: the altar guild workroom. Heaven help the person who messes up the altar guild workroom. You do not trifle with these ladies. The last person to do so was banished to the bell tower. Anyway, I managed to staunch the bleeding and send Wallace back in to the service in time for a flatulence-free performance. As far as I know, the altar guild remains unaware of our trespass.

- It was with great relief when church ended and we were able to go to Saint Wegmans By the Lake and buy modestly priced coffee and muffins.

Back to Reality

Everything is not always wonderful for Wallace in church. Sometimes he has a really bad day, and we have to leave church early. Wallace has trouble with boundaries and sometimes offends people. Wallace often lacks the filter found between brain and mouth. Elisabeth is wonderful at helping Wallace navigate the social intricacies found in church and other places. When Wallace does have trouble, Elisabeth helps him recognize the problem, address the problem, and then move on. We both work hard to help with Wallace's self-esteem.

One of Wallace's most recent, and historic, accomplishments is riding his bicycle in church during the service. Every summer, Saint Luke's sponsors a bike ride around Chautauqua Lake to raise money for the Episcopal Partnership, the diocesan outreach organization. This year, to build up support, I suggested that Wallace ride his bike in church one Sunday during the announcements.

The Loop the Lake leaders loved the idea. I approached our interim rector, who thought it was a fine idea as well. Wallace, of course, could not wait to be the first person to ride his bike in church. Elisabeth and I, knowing our son, arrived early that Sunday to practice. In another first, Wallace was the first person to ride his bike in church while the choir rehearsed. This practice session alone caused more than a few arched eyebrows, but the practice paid off.

Wallace was *on* that morning and rode perfectly. No parishioners or statues were harmed. After church, Wallace received almost overflowing praise and encouragement from the parishioners. Staid old Saint Luke's survived the Great Bike Ride in the Aisles, and Wallace got a great boost of confidence.

Another confidence builder has been the diocesan sleep away camp held every August. This camp is for kids entering third through sixth grades and lasts three and a half days. Sleep away camp takes place at the Lake Chautauqua Lutheran Center, using volunteers from the Episcopal diocese. The first year Wallace attended, he had a good case of the homesick blues. At one point, Wallace packed his bag and announced that he was leaving. The compassionate staff coaxed Wallace into staying, and he ended up enjoying his first camp.

In 2013, Wallace was excited to go back to sleep away camp. Mom's attempt at helping Wallace unpack was met with only perfunctory thanks. Wallace really wanted us to leave. The diocesan youth missioner reported that Wallace sailed every boat in the camp's naval armada. On a couple of occasions, Wallace apparently jumped ship and swam to the next boat.

Wallace was one happy and smelly kid when we picked him up at the end of camp. Elisabeth and I know Wallace had a good time based on the amount of dirt on his shoes, clothes, and body. We had to buy a special brush just to clean his feet and toes. Wallace did have some issues with language and behavior, but the camp staff worked with Wallace to help him succeed.

Another recent event at church showed how Wallace

wants to help even if he is just a kid. A Labor Day storm struck the bell tower at Saint Luke's, causing significant damage. When the construction company hired by the church was appraising the damage, Wallace came out of the parish house and entered into a long conversation with the construction crew. Wallace wanted to know the specific damages and how he could help.

The construction crew was really sweet with Wallace. It was interesting to see these big burly guys bending down to speak with Wallace. In the end, Wallace agreed that he was a little young to help, but he would have if given the chance.

When it comes to anything with Wallace, Elisabeth and I have to have a lot of patience. Wallace will never be the perfect church-attending child. It remains to be seen if Wallace has the self-control to be an acolyte.[33] We try to set reasonable goals and boundaries for Wallace, and our church supports our family. With everyone pitching in, Wallace is learning about his faith and is coming to know God.

---

33 We are not so sure about Wallace carrying a lit candle down the aisle of the church. However, we will give Wallace a chance to prove himself—with an unlit candle of course.

Wallace at the Supper Table and Other Mysteries Explained

Elisabeth and I bought our house in March 2004. I remember the closing fondly: It snowed that day, and as soon as the transaction "went on record," I had to drive over to our new vacant home and shovel the sidewalk. It was the start of a beautiful relationship between me and my snow shovel.

I digress. As we settled in to our new abode, Elisabeth and I realized that we would need a kitchen table to supplement our dining room table. Our house had both an eat-in kitchen and a dining room. We were sort of surprised because it had not been all that long ago that we'd lived in Japan in an apartment smaller than our new attic crawl spaces.

Anyway, in 2004, we really did not have a lot of excess cash and bought an inexpensive table and chairs at Kmart. We thought we would get a nice table in a year or so. The assembly instructions were multilingual in that they had no words, only ill-formed pictures. It took me about three hours swearing like a drunken sailor to put together our new family heirloom. I could already see our descendants fighting with the Smithsonian over the table and chairs.

Flash forward to December 2005 when we bring home Wallace. We knew that, at fourteen months, Wallace would not need a high chair for too long. One of the shower gifts we received was a booster chair with a tray. This became Wallace's spot, or The Seat of Doom. Wallace launched many a vegetable and cookie from this location.

At first, Wallace was so hungry that he would get cranky if you did not feed him fast enough. His pediatrician said let Wallace eat as much as he wants, and we did. A second helping of warm cereal? OK. A third helping? Sure. More fruit? No problem.

It was around this time that we learned that certain foods should be eaten only in moderation. Take raisins, for example. They are nutritious, sweet, and fun to eat. Raisins also are high in fiber, especially when consumed in large quantities. One day, Wallace was his usual starving self and wanted raisins with his supper. He kept asking for more raisins, and we naively let Wallace eat more than a of couple boxes.

"More!"

"What, honey? More raisins?"

(Smiley face)

"OK, here are some raisins."

"Fank you."

We repeated this about three for four times.

"Are we sure that he should eat so many raisins?" Elisabeth asked.

"I don't know. What could go wrong?" I replied, later regretfully.

(Cue the dramatic music.)

Later that night, we all paid the price. You have heard of kids making number 1 or number 2? Wallace made a 3½ that night. It was stunning. We had to call in the county HAZMAT team to contain the situation. The county director of emergency services actually thanked us for giving his team training in biohazard emergencies.[34] Raisins have been banned in our house since 2006.

Even with the occasional over consumption of roughage, Wallace grew enough that we took off the tray to his booster seat. Wallace was now able to sit right at the table with us. You know, the family heirloom. It was about this time that we learned that Wallace was the second coming of Keith Moon and John Bonham. Wallace has banged, pounded, and tapped anything that comes into his grasp. Our table served as the actual drum while the random sippy cup or spoon became drumsticks. What was once a smooth, sleek surface now resembles an old-fashioned washboard.

As Wallace grew, his palate became more refined. In

---

34 No, not really.

other words, macaroni and cheese is now his favorite dish. Kraft Macaroni & Cheese is the standard by which all other pasta dishes are measured. Wallace could write a column on which restaurants in town serve the best and worst macaroni and cheese. Sadly, my own homemade macaroni and cheese would be near the bottom. It seems that Wallace does not prefer using actual cheese in macaroni and cheese.

Wallace's aversion to using real cheese started a few years ago. My parents came to visit and made their annual pilgrimage to Wegmans. Dad bought several varieties of uncommonly pricey cheese that he intended to take home. On the day of departure, Dad dutifully forgot his cheese until he was south of Cleveland.

I certainly was not going to let this highbrow cheese go to waste, so I used the stuff in a big batch of homemade macaroni and cheese. To this day, I tease Dad about how he financed the world's most expensive macaroni and cheese. Wallace was not amused and deemed homemade macaroni and cheese as off limits to anyone under twelve.

Wallace can be a very outgoing young man. He often knows more people at the grocery store than Elisabeth or I do. In many ways, Elisabeth and I feel glad that Wallace feels comfortable engaging in polite conversation. This skill can help Wallace for the rest of his life.

Wallace also possesses a keen sense of curiosity. At age

eleven, Wallace sought to do things that maybe an adult would not. What happens when you stuff popcorn in your nose? What will Mom and Dad do if I wear the same socks for three days in a row?

One recent summer, Wallace decided to conduct a little experiment in a public restaurant. Elisabeth nearly died from embarrassment.

The Taco Hut Affair (Part I)

August signaled that summer was winding down, and Elisabeth and Wallace went to one of our fine local dining establishments, Taco Hut, for lunch. Wallace asked to play a game on Elisabeth's phone as a way to pass the intolerable wait for his three-taco lunch (hard shells with a side of pickles).

Elisabeth let Wallace play his game where he saved planet Earth from zombies and/or girls. The next thing Elisabeth knew, Wallace was standing in the restaurant's kitchen area surrounded by employees. "What did he do now?" thought Elisabeth. As it turns out, Wallace was in search of the Taco Hut Wi-Fi password. Wallace, without any hesitation, marched into the kitchen area and started asking each employee for the Wi-Fi password.

Wallace was only ten and failed to understand the basic concepts of a broom and sweeping. (This has not changed at the ripe old age of twelve.) When it comes to the Interwebs, however, Wallace is fast becoming a little Sheldon Cooper.

Elisabeth apologized profusely to the restaurant staff members, who were actually amused about the situation. "He's cute and entertaining," one waitress said. Book early to have Wallace perform at your holiday party or wedding. Discounts are available to groups of ten or more or if you promise to do Wallace's homework for the night or make macaroni and cheese.

Lunch finally arrived, and Wallace announced that he had to go to the restroom. This is where things turned strange.

The Taco Hut Affair (Part II)

"Mom, I have to go to the bathroom!" exclaimed Wallace, and off he went.

Elisabeth noticed that Wallace stopped at the cashier's desk and asked for a small to-go box before he went to the restroom. *What is he doing?* thought Elisabeth. *What kid takes a to-go box into the restroom?*

Wallace came out of the restroom a few minutes later carrying his white food container. He then spoke to a waitress, who apparently declined Wallace's offer. Another waitress also declined Wallace's offer before Elisabeth could get to him.

Now, you may be thinking the worst right now. It

was after hearing this that I started having chest pains. Elisabeth then told me the full story.

Wallace actually used his restroom time to make some slime using a large quantity of liquid soap and some water. He put his homemade slime into the white food container. Wallace then proceeded to ask the restaurant staff if they wanted to see his slime. Wallace had conversed with two waitresses before Elisabeth was able to dash across the room and intervene.

Actually, Elisabeth was relieved considering what she thought was in the container. Elisabeth escorted Wallace back to their table whereupon they commenced eating. Wallace's white container sat prominently on the table.

Elisabeth and Wallace managed to finish their lunch without any more incidents until they got ready to leave.

As they stepped outside, Wallace opened the container and took out a big handful of slime. "Look, Mom!" he gleefully said.

Elisabeth ordered Wallace to go back inside the Taco Hut and wash his hands while she found the nearest rubbish receptacle for the slime container.

(Some tacos were indeed harmed in bringing you this report.)

Thanksgiving Should Not Start at 4:30 a.m.

Elisabeth and I give thanks for many things in our lives: Wallace, Spam, and Netflix being very high on that roster. Thanksgiving Day is the day we adopted Wallace and brought him home from Russia. We, however, were not so thankful when Wallace woke up at 4:30 a.m. on Thanksgiving morning 2015.

Wallace apparently could not sleep because he was too excited for Thanksgiving. That meant that we all woke up at 4:30 a.m.

"Dad, let's go outside!"

"Not the best idea right now, Son."

"Mom, will you make me breakfast now?"

"After the sun comes up, I will."

"Hey, guys, I want to dress up for Thanksgiving!"

"OK, but let's wait about six hours to get dressed."

"Ohh, man!" (not Wallace's exact words)

I managed to convince Wallace that he and I should go downstairs to let Elisabeth try to sleep some more. Sometimes, a dad must take one for the team. Wallace and I enjoyed some quality Disney Channel time, though I did have to nix the pre-dawn consumption of M&Ms. ADHD and RAD add a whole new facet to a family's life.

Elisabeth came downstairs some time later ready for

battle—umm, ready to make pumpkin pies. Though we were not hosting Thanksgiving dinner, Elisabeth had the honor of making her mother's pumpkin chiffon pie. Elisabeth made two pies to take to two different family dinners. The Rankins were on the Thanksgiving Food Circuit that year.

The recipe for pumpkin chiffon pie calls for the cook to separate multiple egg whites. It was during this point in the process that Wallace decided that he needed to show Mom something other than egg whites. Elisabeth quite pointedly stated that Wallace should immediately leave the kitchen or else be prepared to eat spinach for the rest of his life.

Feeling unloved, Wallace then proceeded to go up to his room whereupon he finally went back to sleep. I then did the only thing possible at this point: I went to Elisabeth's favorite place for coffee and got her a large "1&1"[35] to go.

Wallace, mercifully, slept for a couple of hours, and Elisabeth had her favorite coffee. Life on Arlington Avenue quieted down for a while.

All good things must come to an end, and Wallace eventually woke up from his nap. He woke up ready to get dressed for Thanksgiving. To his credit, Wallace wanted to look handsome for the special day.

Elisabeth and I managed to dress ourselves without the

---

35 That's one cream and one sugar in coffee speak.

need of a committee. Elisabeth looked as beautiful as ever while I went for the semi-formal woodsman look.

With pumpkin chiffon pie and cucumber-based appetizers in hand, the Rankin family departed for the one-mile trip to dine with Elisabeth's sister and her family.

Wallace had a fun time with his older cousins and played a mean game of football while wearing his formal ensemble. (No button-down shirts were harmed in bringing you this report.) However, Wallace showed that he could catch a touchdown pass while still keeping his necktie smartly centered on his shirt.

(Some people wonder why we let Wallace play football while wearing a suit. Elisabeth and I decided that we can always wash clothes, but fun memories seemed more important on this particular day.)

We later drove over to another dinner hosted by Elisabeth's niece. Elisabeth and I did not eat much, but Wallace partook of the traditional Thanksgiving chips and salsa. We ended the day relatively early. ADHD, RAD and lack of sleep can take a toll on a kid (and parents).

This was not the most exciting Thanksgiving for the Rankin family. On the other hand, our family was together, and Wallace enjoyed the holiday even if he woke up three hours before sunrise. Nothing makes Elisabeth and me happier than seeing our son enjoy himself despite all of the challenges he faces in life.

Life through Social Media

I joined Facebook in 2009 as a way to stay in touch with friends and family in far-off lands, like Cleveland. Elisabeth joined in 2013 after spending four years of reading over my shoulder. My initial posts were bland and not very illuminating. I then posted a couple of stories about Wallace and found an outlet to share our experiences as a family.

I have expanded some posts to put things in context. Other posts stand on their own. Either way, these snippets provide a glimpse inside Rankin House.

I start off with an episode that occurred during one of Wallace's culinary adventures. Wallace wants to be independent but forgets that he is only twelve, nine in the following story. Enough time has passed. The horror is but a memory. The story can finally be told.

2014

The Great Cocoa Powder Spill of 2014

Master Wallace wanted to make some hot cocoa one day earlier this summer. After carefully measuring the cocoa powder, sugar, and milk, Wallace went to put away the ingredients. Using all the fine motor skills of a nine-year-old boy, Wallace tried to put away the cocoa powder. The container slipped from his grasp. Calamity ensued. The scene is etched into my memory like the 1986 World Series: horror.

There was cocoa powder everywhere in the kitchen. Wallace's arms and upper torso were covered in cocoa soot. Wallace had opened the door to the spice cabinet, home to the cocoa powder, and every spice container now contained the dreaded brown powder. A cocoa powder fog had descended upon the kitchen.

Mom jumped into action and quickly contained the damage. Boy, counter, and floor were soon reasonably clean. The spice cabinet took another day. In the aftermath, we had to put the dustpan in the dishwasher in order to get it clean.

Wallace now has a pair of wide receiver "sticky gloves" for use in the kitchen.

Time to Wake Up Dept.

Wallace and the dog both decided to wake up at 6:15 this morning. So much for Sleep-in Saturday. I think I will wake Wallace up at this hour on Monday and see how *he* feels.

(Wallace did not appreciate at all waking up at 7:15 a.m. the next Monday. In fact, only the dog was interested in getting up that day.)

Two Scenes from a Spring Weekend

1. Wallace and Elisabeth put their heads together on Saturday to plan the most efficient route to hit all of the yard sales in the neighborhood. I think Wallace is a more cunning negotiator than Elisabeth. (The dog and I stayed home. One of us drank a beer.)
2. Wallace exited his Sunday school lesson with glue on the back of his head. We still have not received a clear explanation. The most entertaining version had all of the girls plotting to take over and Wallace leading a valiant charge of the boys.

2014 Spring Concert Tour

Wallace played in the Chautauqua Regional Youth Symphony (Prelude Strings) concert this afternoon. On his own one and a half hours before the concert, Wallace started getting dressed. He wanted to "look perfect" for his concert. Our special little guy hears, "No," far too often in his young life. It was so great to see Wallace perform with the other talented/ambitious children today.

You don't know music until you've heard the Prelude Strings.

Wallace's Violin Concert Tour— Update

Last night, Wallace and a big bunch of other young musicians performed with the Western New York Chamber Orchestra. It was really fun to see a professional orchestra and children all on stage playing songs such as "Mississippi Hotdog." Wallace personified "Ode to Joy" after the concert by doing cartwheels outside the auditorium. We enjoyed a post-concert celebration at Friendly's where there was mac and cheese aplenty. (No musicians, gymnasts, or waitresses were harmed in bringing you this report.)

Wallace Meets the New Priest (Are You Wallace-Experienced?)

Yesterday, Saturday, Wallace went to visit a classmate at his house. A great time was had by all. Wallace's young classmate even gave Wallace his pet toad. (There was no parental consultation.) When Mom went to pick up Wallace, Mom got to meet the new addition to the Rankin family. Joy in Mudville?

Our new rector (priest) and his wife arrived Thursday. Elisabeth (i.e., Mom) thought it might be nice to stop by the rectory (one of those funky Episcopal words) and offer move-in assistance. Apparently, Father Luke and Willow, his wife, had received the Wallace Briefing. It was no surprise then when Elisabeth and Wallace showed up with a toad in tow to meet our new rector.

Father Luke and Willow were very welcoming and gracious. Wallace thereupon entered into a theoretical discussion regarding Heaven. (Really.) Elisabeth then convinced Wallace to make a strategic withdrawal and avoid subjecting the rector and wife to the full-on Wallace Experience.

Spring Break 2014

Wallace got to spend Thursday morning working as a junior zoo keeper. He had lots of fun. Wallace insisted on trying all of the animal food, including the peanut shells. At bedtime, he complained of a slight tummy ache. Wallace learned that spaghetti makes a better meal than fortified grain pellets and peanut shells. (No actual zoo keepers were harmed in bringing you this report.)

Out of the Mouths of Babes Dept.

Tonight, Wallace opined on how to become a school principal:

- Do not get "wedgied" on the first day of school.
- Learn all of the kids' names.
- Set up your office.
- Help the teachers.
- Learn how to talk loudly.
- If you have to suspend a student, let them down gently.

Floyd Nightingale Dept.

Elisabeth was under the weather this past weekend. Wallace wanted to help Mom and thought she needed some snacks. First, he made some melted cheese for Mom, then Wallace made some saltine crackers and melted marshmallow sandwiches for her. I give Elisabeth credit for praising Wallace while being revolted at the same time. Apparently, Wallace wants to become a dietician when he grows up.

Abstract Number Dept.

This really happened:

Son: Dad, guess what number I am thinking in my head.

Dad: Three?

Son: No.

Dad: Twenty-nine?

Son: No

Dad: Two hundred and twenty-five?

Son: No.

Dad: Well, what is it?

Son: Infinity minus one.

Dad: You aren't playing fair.

Son: (laughs)

Call Me Wallace Dept.

Tonight, we discussed the plot of *Moby Dick* and how it compares to that of *Free Willy*. Call me Wallace.

(Wallace really did ask me about *Moby Dick* and *Free Willy*. I am not sure at all where he came with this question. Apparently, Wallace is a well-read nine-year-old boy.)

2013

Checking It Out Dept.

Wallace checked out *The Dangerous Book For Boys* from the school library and promptly started learning the Navajo Code Talker language. The first Navajo Code word he memorized was "jackass." The life a nine-year-old boy.

This book actually did teach kids the word "jackass." Wallace's teacher at first wanted to chastise Wallace for saying such a word in class but backed off once Wallace pointed out that the book came from the school library.

Not Specific Enough Dept.

The scene: A quiet residential street in scenic Jamestown, NY. We are inside the house of an unusually good-looking family.

The cast: A wonderful mom and an adoring child.

Mom: (slightly annoyed) Oh, will you just get in the car right now!

Son: I'm going, I'm going.

Later, at the entrance to the violin teacher's studio:

Mom: Where are your shoes?!?

Son: You didn't tell me I had to wear shoes to violin practice.

Mom turns to the audience: That rascal!

Elisabeth reported that Wallace indeed went to violin practice without his shoes. We then instituted the rule that, when outside the house, shoes must we worn whenever you wear clothes.

Aliens Took My Child Dept.

Last night, I made Wallace a cheeseburger and warmed up some broccoli for supper. (Elisabeth was at choir practice, so we had bachelor night.) Wallace ate his broccoli, quite willingly, but did not want his cheeseburger. In other news, Hades reported widespread frost.

Ready for the Apocalypse?!?

When Elisabeth checked on Wallace last night, she found him sound asleep with the following items in his bed: seven volumes in the *Captain Underpants* series, a glow stick, Magic 8 Ball, and an old cell phone.

Our Little Philosopher

Tonight, when I arrived home, Wallace was doing his impression of a water sprinkler: he was holding a water can and spinning in a circle.

A little later, Wallace told me to "loosen up and live a little, Dad!" Wallace told Mom, "Haven't you ever wanted to sit on a cloud on a warm summer day?"

Trying to Tell Me Something Dept.

Wallace's teacher rewards her students with points for good behavior. Every Friday, his teacher opens her store, and the kids can buy things with their points. Wallace usually buys toys, sometimes a present for Mom. Today, Wallace thought to buy me a present that I apparently needed: some Right Guard deodorant. Through my laughter, I managed to thank my son.

2012

Christmas 2012

Wallace has made his official Naughty and Nice List. Not only am I on the naughty side, but Wallace pointed out that he wrote my name with permanent ink. Mom is on the little-known Undecided List.

How Mom Got Her Phone Back

We were home watching a family movie when Wallace's babysitter stopped by with Mom's phone. It seems that someone saw Mom's phone at the Family Dollar store and saw Wallace's picture on the screen. That person apparently said, "Hey, that's Wallace Rankin!" Amazingly, this person knows Wallace's babysitter and gave the phone to her. Wallace's status as a minor celebrity paid off for Elisabeth. Next week, Wallace will be the guest host on Conan.

The Kindest Rejection Dept.

I made dinner the other night, and apparently Wallace did not want to hurt my feelings:

"Dad, you did a good job with dinner tonight, and I know

you worked hard. Thank you for cooking. But I just don't care for it."

Two Bachelor Guys Dept.

Mom was away this weekend visiting friends. Wallace and I were left to ourselves. We partook in lots of Chinese food and SpongeBob. Wallace then decided that we needed to bake a cake to surprise Mom tonight when she got home. Some of the cake batter actually made it into the pan. Some of the frosting actually landed on the cake. Mom was happy even though the cake did not look much like a cake.

Embarrass Your Child Dept.

For family time tonight, we watched *Back at the Barnyard* on Nickelodeon. Elisabeth and I started dancing during the closing credits. It was a dance floor of awesomeness.

Wallace, on the other hand, had this to say: "My eyes! They Burn!"

Too bad we do not have a video of all this.

The Dog Was Not That Interested

Happy Eighth Birthday to Wallace! Master Wallace decided to get up at 6 a.m. today (over an hour earlier than normal). He came into the parental bedroom at this unjust hour and commenced a conversation with our dog. Elisabeth and I got to watch the sun rise while listening to Wallace and Chip discuss the merits of SpongeBob. Happy Birthday.

A Personal Best at School Dept.?

Wallace started the third grade today. His first talk with the principal was thirty minutes after school started.

Shadow Puppets Dept.

Wallace and I went to see *Madagascar 3* at the Chautauqua Mall Cinema yesterday. During the movie, Wallace twice asked to use the restroom. I did not think much of this until the second trip when I saw a shadow flicker across the screen. Yes, the projection booth was unattended, and yes, Wallace thought it a fine place to visit without adult supervision. (I notified the management of their open door policy.)

Grammar Dept.

Son: I don't watch *Family Guy* because it's crap.

Dad: Use the word "inappropriate" instead.

Son: I don't watch *Family Guy* because it's inappropriate crap.

Dad: How about those Red Sox?

Open Mic Night

Last night, we went to the open house at Rogers Elementary School. Elisabeth and I were talking with another parent when we heard Wallace on the school PA system: "Will my Dad please report to the principal's office!"

It seems someone left the school office unguarded, and Wallace saw an opportunity for mischief.

Many people remember that little incident. People would come up to us everywhere we went to ask if Wallace really took over the school PA system, Elisabeth and I thought it funny, and it was hard to talk to Wallace without laughing.

Tough Guy Dept.

Darth Maul unleashes a devastating attack on Iron Man, but Iron Man dodges in the nick of time.

Dad: Wallace, it's time to come inside for supper.

Son: Dad, Darth Maul doesn't eat supper.

Dad: If Darth Maul wants ice cream later, he will.

Son: OK.

Mr. Charm and Personality Dept.

The Place: The white house with blue shutters

The Time: 7:20 a.m.

Dad: Time to get up, Son.

Son: WHO DARES DISTURB MY SLUMBER!

Dad: That would be me, the guy making your breakfast today.

Son: AAARRRRGHHH!

(In the end, the promise of breakfast helped capture the raging beast.)

A Child's Love in the Twenty-First Century

Wallace announced last night that if he becomes a zombie, then he will NOT eat Mom's brains or my brains.

Neil Peart Dept.

Wallace and I went to see the wonderful Chautauqua Chamber Singers concert tonight. The added bonus was watching Mom up on the stage with the other sopranos. Those that attended the post-concert reception got to hear Wallace give an impromptu free-form drum solo on the unattended drum set. (We quickly exited after that.)

The concert took place in a local church. The reception was downstairs in the church basement. The church band had left their instruments, and Wallace seized the opportunity to show us his percussion skills.

Mr. Sympathy?

Son: Dad, are you a spy?
Dad: No, I am a lawyer.
Son: Sorry, Dad.

Breaking News Dept.

At lunch today, Wallace announced that he is a ninja who fights bad guys at night when we are sleeping. Wallace also stated that his ninja name is Mike.

For the next twenty-four hours or so, Wallace demanded that we call him Mike when in public. Elisabeth and I still scratch our heads over this announcement.

Not Helpful Dept.

In 2010, Elisabeth and I had a talk with Wallace about bathroom hygiene. The talk did not go as Elisabeth had planned.

Mom: Son, we do not pee in the bathtub.

Dad: That's right, we pee in the shower.

Mom: You can sleep on the porch tonight, Dad.

Wallace's Continuing Search for A Frog

Wallace has wanted his very own pet for years. Aside from a tragic experiment with goldfish, Elisabeth and I have not really wanted another pet in the house. We have said no to the following proposed pets: a second dog, a second cat, a guinea pig, a monkey, a snake, a frog, and a scorpion.

Wallace keeps trying though. Our local community college owns a wooded park near our house. A stream runs right through this park, and it is a favorite spot of Wallace's. In this quest of Wallace's, as in others, best laid plans have gone astray.

We went to a graduation party today at a local park. Wallace found a little frog and wanted to protect it. By "protect," Wallace meant put the frog in my car, along with my car keys, and then locked my car. Thank goodness for AAA. You can now contact Wallace at Father O'Connor's

Home for Wayward Boys.

About an hour later, AAA showed up and had my car open in about thirty seconds. The frog survived, and we returned it to its home by the creek. The incident with my car led to one of my most favorite interactions with Wallace, which occurred later the same day:

Wallace: Dad, can I have the keys to your car?

Dad: No.

Wallace: Crap! (*Wallace dejectedly walked away.*)

I wonder what he would have done if I had said yes.

In 2014, Wallace still wanted a frog or toad. One day, he convinced one of his behavioral counselors to take him to a local pet store. Frogs cost only about $6, but the "containment costs" far exceeded the cost of a frog. That started a running search for a toad or frog.

Wallace and the Toad

As I mentioned in an earlier post, Wallace's young friend recently gave him a toad. The look on Elisabeth's face must have been priceless. After their visit to meet our new rector and his wife, Wallace received a message that his young friend was having extreme "giver's remorse." Apparently, nine-year-old boys have trouble with the concept of thinking things through. Wallace, all on his own, made one of the most mature decisions of his young life: Wallace chose to bring back the toad to his now upset friend.

Wallace was sad but confident in his decision. Summoning all of her motherly courage, Elisabeth then took Wallace on a toad hunting expedition. Wallace had showed great maturity, and Mom wanted to reward him. Off they went to the 100-Acre Park near our house. Wallace had a great time hunting for toads in the stream and mud. Alas, The Great Toad Migration of 2014 had passed, and there were no toads to be found. In the end, Wallace had a good day and was quite happy. Elisabeth and I are proud of our son and pleased that we missed The Great Toad Migration of 2014.

Scenes From Another Spring Afternoon

It was a lazy Sunday afternoon. Mom was running errands, so Wallace and I went to the local creek to continue the Great Toad Hunt of 2014. Sadly, there were no toads, frogs, or any other amphibians to be found. Wallace then drowned his sorrows in an ice cream cone. Now, we are relaxing watching the philosophical musings of *iCarly*.

At Saint Luke's annual picnic in June (2014), we once again went up to Camp Onyahsa on Chautauqua Lake. One of the parishioners brought his two snakes along to show the kids. Once again, Elisabeth and I had to put the kibosh on any type of snake taking up residence in Rankin House. On a positive note, no anti-venom was needed that afternoon.

The Trip to Toys "R" Us

"The ice is really bad, honey. We may have to turn around," said Mom.

A relatively uncommon ice storm had moved through the area, and driving on the interstate was not easy. Then Mom looked at Wallace.

The story had started earlier that morning.

"Mom, can we go to Toys 'R' Us today?" said Wallace, his face showing an earnest plea yet not wanting to be let down.

Scenic Jamestown does not have all the retail establishments commonly found in other areas. Local residents literally cheered when the fine dining Panera establishment finally opened here. One store the Jamestown area still lacks is a Toys "R" Us.

"Sure, honey. Get your gift card."

Wallace had never been to a Toys "R" Us, and visiting the store had become a real dream for him. This past Christmas, Wallace's grandparents gave him a Toys "R" Us gift card. On the last Saturday of winter vacation, Wallace and Mom decided to drive to the big city of Erie (Pennsylvania) to go to the Toys "R" Us there.

There were a few cars that had slid off the road. Mom told Wallace that they might have to turn back because the roads might not be safe. Wallace looked at Mom, sighed heavily, and conceded, "I understand, Mom."

He held his Toys "R" Us gift card in his hand like it was a gift from Heaven. Wallace's face could not mask the extreme disappointment and sadness.

Have you ever come close to fulfilling a lifelong dream only to fail at the very end?

Mom saw the look on Wallace's face and pressed on. They made it safely, if slowly, to Erie. There are no words to really express the pure joy on Wallace's face as they pulled up to the Toys "R" Us. "We made it!" said Wallace as he bounded out of the car.

Wallace and Mom stayed in Erie for a while as the temperature climbed above freezing. Wallace used his gift card for some cool stuff. Wallace also thought about Mom and Dad bought them each a small toy.

Wallace had also brought along a McDonald's gift card that he had saved. "Mom, let me get your coffee today. Thanks for taking me to Toys 'R' Us," said one happy boy.

A Family of Three for Eleven Years

As I write this chapter, the last eleven years seem like a blur, yet we are still a family. Life goes on for us. Of course, we have no choice in the matter. Wallace is in the sixth grade as I write this chapter and has periods where everything seems really wonderful. Wallace, sadly, also has periods where he struggles with his mental health.

Elisabeth, Wallace, and I are all lucky that we completed the adoption process before things changed. The Russian government, in 2012, banned US citizens adopting Russian children. This ban continues today as far as I know. The reason for the ban depends on whom you ask. Certainly, Russian pride and nationalism is part of the reason. Some very rare, but disturbing stories of failed adoptions in the U.S. also played a role in the ban. What saddens me the most is that I do not think domestic Russian adoptions have increased all that much.[36]

---

36 Alexandra Tyan, "The Russian Parents Challenging Stigma Surrounding Adoption," *The Guardian*, August 31, 2015, http://www. theguardian.com/world/2015/aug/31/russia-adoption-stigma-ban, last checked on February 25, 2017.

Another lucky aspect of our adoption is that our adoption agency had the decency not to close under dubious circumstances until after Wallace had come home. I doubt this was intentional on the part of our adoption agency, but I will gladly accept beneficial coincidental timing. The thought of our adoption agency closing in between our trips to Russia, after we had met Wallace, still causes me great anxiety.

Amrex's bankruptcy also took place after we had brought Wallace home. Elisabeth and I really did not have any way to independently make the necessary contacts in Kemerovo in order to complete the adoption process. How would that work? The Google search would have been something like this "People in Kemerovo who speak English and are willing to help a married couple from Jamestown, New York (USA) adopt a baby." The failure of Amrex alone hurt many people hoping to adopt children from Russia.

Unquestionably, Elisabeth and I were hardly prepared for what awaited us and Wallace. His special needs did not become prevalent until over a year after we had returned to Jamestown. Even then, we recognized only the ADHD symptoms and not the RAD symptoms until much later. Some of the mistakes we made as parents seem so glaring now. Elisabeth and I wish we could get a do-over for some of these mistakes.

When we see Wallace struggle with everyday life, Elisabeth and I weep inside and outside. We get upset with Wallace when he acts disrespectfully or uses physical aggression to show his anger. At the same time, Elisabeth and I remember that Wallace is a young boy with delayed brain development. Balancing our emotions with our (limited) understanding of Wallace's brain disorders is not easy. Elisabeth and I keep trying. Most importantly, so does Wallace.

We love Wallace and do not regret at all our decision to adopt him. Wallace is a sweet young man with a huge heart. Wallace loves to help younger kids in school, and he can actually show great sympathy when he sees children and adults in need.

Wallace also wants to experience everything he can in life. From tasting his shampoo every day to trying new ramps at the skateboard park to making fruit smoothies for the family, Wallace wants to see and do as much as possible. Wallace possesses a keen intellect and sense of humor. Wallace can hold his own in conversations with adults.

Wallace's story—our family's story—does not end here. Wallace may have reached the ripe old age of twelve, but he has many years of life to live. Finishing middle school and high school will challenge our entire family. On the social side, Wallace already knows how to charm girls and women. That part of Wallace's journey could very well form the basis of a sequel to this book.

I hope that I have achieved my goals in this book. I hope that people take a more understanding and nuanced view of mental illness, especially with children. I talk about this more in the supplemental chapter that follows, but the point bears repeating: Physical delays in brain development can cause significant behavioral issues in children. Just because you cannot see a child's brain does not make the physical delay imaginary. The resultant behaviors don't make the child *bad* any more than a child with asthma is *bad*. When you see children diagnosed with ADHD or Reactive Attachment Disorder, understand that these kids have very real neurological disorders.

I also hope that I have shown a realistic, but mostly positive, view of international adoptions. There are many children in this world that need adoptive parents. There are many people who work tirelessly to match children in need with adoptive parents. Maybe our adoption story is not exactly the same as other families' adoption stories, but I think roller coasters of emotions, bureaucratic hassles, and (hopefully) ultimate joy are common to all families with adopted children.

For people who live in Jamestown, I hope you understand Wallace a little more. Wallace's growth and development follow a circuitous route, and that frustrates some people, including Elisabeth and me. We need to have different expectations for children with special needs. Love, understanding, and encouragement really do work wonders for kids like Wallace. Yes, we hold Wallace accountable as well. Elisabeth and I always say to Wallace, "You are always responsible for your actions even if you do not always intend your actions."

I hope you enjoyed this book. Please read the supplemental chapter to learn a little more about AHDD and RAD. My crystal ball is at the dry cleaners today, and I cannot really say what will happen next. Whatever happens, Wallace will make life very interesting, and Elisabeth and I will love Wallace (and each other).

ADHD and RAD—A Brief Introduction

Wallace is really the joy in our lives, but his mental health issues are significant. The purpose of this chapter is to:

- Give a short explanation of ADHD and RAD to the extent a fortysomething father can;
- Try to remove the stigma of mental health treatment; and
- Make you look up the terms, *caudate nucleus* and *Spam musubi*.

(Controversial Medical Science Ahead)

If you are reading this section seeking a definitive explanation of ADHD and RAD, then you will be learning, not from a medical professional but an attorney moonlighting as an author. If you are reading this chapter because you have a homework assignment on ADHD or RAD, then you will probably get a B- on your assignment.

As previously stated, however, my goal here is to explain, from a parent's perspective, what these two disorders mean for the Rankin family. ADHD is short for Attention

Deficit/Hyperactivity Disorder. RAD is short for Reactive Attachment Disorder. Because I am not rewarded in any way by using extra syllables, I will use the abbreviations for these terms.

ADHD—It Is Not Imaginary

Attention Deficit/Hyperactivity Disorder is a disorder of the brain. ADHD is a very real problem for children and adults. When I first learned of ADHD (then called ADD), I thought it meant that parents were not paying enough attention to their kids. They lacked attention. It seemed so simple, and I could not understand why kids needed medication so their parents would pay attention to them. I was wrong about that[37] and have tried to learn more about ADHD.

At this point, I will be referring to the National Institutes of Mental Health (NIMH), which is part of the National Institutes of Health. The NIMH is a US government institute whose stated mission is to "transform the understanding and treatment of mental illnesses through basic and clinical research, paving the way for prevention, recovery, and cure."[38] The NIMH has, and continues, to

37 I also think the first *Star Wars* prequel is not as bad as people think.

38 http://www.nimh.nih.gov/about/index.shtml, last checked on February 25, 2017.

extensively research ADHD's causes and treatments.

The NIMH website puts the neurological causes of ADHD in a very succinct paragraph, which I now shamelessly quote:

"Brain imaging studies have revealed that, in youth with ADHD, the brain matures in a normal pattern but is delayed, on average, by about 3 years. The delay is most pronounced in brain regions involved in thinking, paying attention, and planning. More recent studies have found that the outermost layer of the brain, the cortex, shows delayed maturation overall, and a brain structure important for proper communications between the two halves of the brain shows an abnormal growth pattern. These delays and abnormalities may underlie the hallmark symptoms of ADHD and help to explain how the disorder may develop."[39]

If I correctly understand the above explanation, a child with ADHD has a brain that matures more slowly than a child without ADHD. Eventually, the brain of a child with ADHD does catch up with overall maturation of his/her entire body. The cortex part of the brain, however, may show an abnormal growth pattern.

Another NIMH publication goes into great detail about

---

39 http://www.nimh.nih.gov/health/publications/attention-deficit-hyperactivity-disorder/index.shtml, last checked on February 25, 2017. The NIMH website has three citations within this paragraph, which I removed to keep the explanation less cluttered.

the brain and ADHD. I will now impress you with a quote from this publication:

"Imaging studies have reported reduced volume of the caudate nucleus, and particularly parts of the cerebellum in ADHD."[40]

I do not really know what this means other than ADHD is a *physical disorder* of the brain. That is the takeaway from this section.

The tough part as a parent is not being able to see the physical issue with the brain. You can easily see a child with a broken arm or a child who is small for his or her age. A parent, unless he or she is a neurologist with horribly expensive imaging equipment at home, cannot see a slowly maturing brain. There is a temptation, as a parent, to imprecisely think of ADHD as some sort of generic label for kids who cannot sit still.

What are the symptoms we can see in children with ADHD? Below is a list of common behaviors and symptoms:[41]

---

40 http://www.ncbi.nlm.nih.gov/pmc/articles/PMC2863119/, last checked on February 25, 2017. The NIMH website had two citations for this one sentence, which I removed to keep this explanation less cluttered.

41 http://www.nimh.nih.gov/health/publications/attention-deficit-hyperactivity-disorder/index.shtml#pub2, last checked on February 25, 2017.

Children who have symptoms of inattention may:

- Be easily distracted, miss details, forget things, and frequently switch from one activity to another
- Have difficulty focusing on one thing
- Become bored with a task after only a few minutes, unless they are doing something enjoyable
- Have difficulty focusing attention on organizing and completing a task or learning something new
- Have trouble completing or turning in homework assignments, often losing things (e.g., pencils, toys, assignments) needed to complete tasks or activities
- Not seem to listen when spoken to
- Daydream, become easily confused, and move slowly
- Have difficulty processing information as quickly and accurately as others
- Struggle to follow instructions.

Children who have symptoms of hyperactivity may:

- Fidget and squirm in their seats
- Talk nonstop
- Dash around, touching or playing with anything and everything in sight
- Have trouble sitting still during dinner, school, and story time
- Be constantly in motion
- Have difficulty doing quiet tasks or activities.

Children who have symptoms of impulsivity may:

- Be very impatient
- Blurt out inappropriate comments, show their emotions without restraint, and act without regard for consequences
- Have difficulty waiting for things they want or waiting their turns in games
- Often interrupt conversations or others' activities.

That brings me back to Wallace and his legendary inability to remain still. Most days, Wallace seems to be in constant motion. Wallace, for example, cannot sit still while watching television. He rocks back and forth (when not sitting next to either Elisabeth or me) so much that he burns more calories in thirty minutes than most people burn at the gym on any given day.

Elisabeth and I constantly have to remind ourselves that Wallace's brain is wired differently than other kids of his age. Sometimes, we want to say, "Stop it!" but Wallace cannot always do that. We have learned techniques like holding his hand or rubbing his back to help Wallace stay calm. While we have the benefit of Wallace's counselors, Elisabeth and I also learn by trial and error. Sometimes it feels mostly like error.

A friend of ours, who is a special education teacher, once said: "With kids like Wallace, if you ask them to sit down and be quiet, what you are really saying is chose one or the other." Sometimes this seems quite true. Elisabeth and I keep trying to get to both goals, but we know this will take a lot of time.

How do you treat kids with ADHD? I will get to medications in a moment. However, the foundations of treatment, in my opinion, are A) parent education and B) therapy/counseling for the child. The more the parents understand ADHD, the better the parents are at helping their child or children. Likewise, professional counseling and therapy help guide the child (and parents) into making positive choices. Before Wallace can choose to react with positive choices, he must have a mental list of positive options. A good ADHD counselor can help a child develop an individual mental list of positive options and choices.

Medication is not the cure, but medication helps. Without parental education and therapy/counseling for the child, then the medication will only be partially effective. I do not understand why low doses of stimulants help ADHD kids slow down, but they work. Apparently, certain stimulants work in the areas of the brain that support attention and focused behavior.[42] For Wallace, the medications help him slow down with his schoolwork and pay attention in class.

---

42 http://www.nimh.nih.gov/health/publications/attention-deficit-hyperactivity-disorder/index.shtml#pub5, last checked February 25, 2017.

Two of the main side effects of Wallace's ADHD medications are difficulty sleeping and lack of appetite. Wallace's ADHD is so profound that he was diagnosed at age three. He takes a healthy dose of ADHD medications every day. Consequently, he takes some other medications to help him sleep at night, but these medications are not sleeping pills like Ambien.

The lack of appetite is also very common in ADHD kids. I have seen very few overweight ADHD children. We try to time his medications around meals, but Wallace's food intake is sporadic. Wallace will make up for lost meals at some point in the day or week. For example, I took Wallace out to breakfast the other morning so Elisabeth could have some time alone.[43] He ate a kid's serving of pancakes and then half a cheese omelet. On other mornings, Wallace will not even finish a piece of toast.

ADHD makes life challenging for Wallace. He goes a mile a minute even when taking his medications. His counseling has taken time, but we can now see Wallace choosing to not act impulsively on occasion. The counseling also helps Wallace become self-aware, and he recognizes, more frequently now, the need to think about his choices. Unfortunately, Wallace also has another diagnosis.

---

43 Bob Evans Restaurant if you are keeping track.

RAD Does Not Mean "Radical"

Reactive Attachment Disorder is a serious condition that develops in children who did not have a chance to bond with a parent or parent substitute at birth. More pertinently, a child who was orphaned before establishing a parental bond has a good chance for developing RAD. I understand that an infant must receive basic comfort, affection, and nurturing in order to learn to establish loving and caring relationships with other people.[44] I also look at RAD as the result of early childhood trauma—the lack of a meaningful parental bond.

RAD is also a byproduct of abnormal brain growth and is in the middle of the nature vs. nurture argument (in my opinion). A newborn infant needs to attach with at least one parent in order to develop socially. The lack of a nurturing attachment, where both parent and child attach to each other, can cause negative psychological consequences in childhood and adult life.[45] This lack of

---

44 http://en.wikipedia.org/wiki/Reactive_attachment_disorder#cite_note-2, last checked on February 25, 2017.

45 Harvey A. Weinberg, "Improved Functioning in Children Diagnosed With Reactive Attachment Disorder After SSRI Treatment," *Journal of the Canadian Academy of Child and Adolescent Psychiatry* (2010), http://www.ncbi.nlm.nih.gov/pmc/articles/PMC2809447/, last checked on February 25, 2017.

attachment can lead to hormonal and neurotransmitter deficiencies in a child with RAD.[46] Another study by Dr. Allan Schore has shown that failure of an infant to establish a nurturing attachment to an adult caregiver can negatively influence the development of the right side of the child's brain.[47] Dr. Schore concludes, in part, that the brain's physical development is greatly influenced by exterior social communication.[48]

I am not for a moment going to suggest that I fully understand these detailed scientific papers. My goal also does not include conducting original research into brain development and RAD. I, however, hopefully make the case that RAD is both a physical affliction of the brain and a very serious psychiatric illness.

There is a whole list of RAD symptoms, but I want to focus on two areas: "pull away" behaviors and "everyone is my friend" behaviors.[49] The confounding thing about RAD is that the same child can have behaviors from both areas at the same time.

---

46 Ibid.

47 Allan N. Schore, "The Effects of a Secure Attachment Relationship on Right Brain Development, Affect Regulation, and Infant Mental Health," *Infant Mental Health Journal 22*, (2001): 1-2, 7–66.

48 Ibid, 11.

49 http://en.wikipedia.org/wiki/Reactive_attachment_disorder#cite_note-2, last checked on February 25, 2017.

Pull away behavior is basically shunning relationships and attachments with others.[50] Everyone is my friend behavior is the opposite: Children seek the attention of everyone, including strangers. RAD children may express an overfamiliarity with strangers or lack any specificity with regards to selection of attachment figures.[51] For example, Wallace and I went to the grocery store the other day. Without any warning, Wallace struck up a pleasant conversation with the lady behind us, whom neither of us knew. They ended up talking about their Christmas holiday plans like they were old friends. This aspect of RAD could actually help Wallace in the future, but it scares Elisabeth and me when he indiscriminately picks out new friends.

Wallace frequently strikes up conversations with strangers. He can be very sociable and charming on occasion. The adage "A stranger is a friend you have not met yet" is not always accurate in real life, and we regularly discuss with Wallace the concept of *stranger danger*. The balancing act is teaching Wallace to see and observe personal boundaries while encouraging him to be polite and social.

RAD is a very difficult diagnosis for a child. RAD, in my opinion, often means that the child cannot bond with a parent in such a way that the child has extreme difficulty

---

50 Ibid.

51 Ibid.

with *any* type of relationship. Some days, Wallace wants nothing to do with me or Elisabeth. This behavior also spills over to Wallace's interactions with his teachers and classmates. It is very difficult to accept this behavior as a symptom of RAD, and we swallow hard quite a lot.

It is hard to adequately describe what life is like for a family that has a child with a RAD diagnosis. When I say Wallace pulls away, it is often abrupt and emotional. To an outsider, it may look like a petulant, disrespectful child. Often, though, there is a lot going on with the RAD child, and it is not fair to simply call him disrespectful. Wallace never bonded with his birth mother, and that makes it very difficult for him to maintain relationships with Elisabeth and me (and others).

Do not think, however, that we give Wallace a pass on inappropriate behavior. A RAD child having a meltdown will most likely not be able to respond to corrective instruction until after the crisis has abated. Then, we talk about what happened, why it happened, and the consequences. We tell Wallace that he is responsible for his behavior even if he did not intend the behavior. However, this might mean we leave the restaurant, go home, and then have a chance to calmly discuss the event and what the consequence will be. Our fellow restaurant patrons do not see the whole process, only the "bad behavior."

RAD also has an anxiety component. Counseling, and

to a certain extent medications, help address Wallace's RAD-related anxiety. Elisabeth and I frequently tell Wallace that we love him. We frequently reiterate that we are not going away and that Wallace deserves to have a good life. We usually let Wallace fall asleep with the door to his room open. Wallace does not sleep well when either Elisabeth or I are not home at bedtime. Wallace needs frequent hugs from us, and we return the embrace. Elisabeth and I try very hard to let Wallace know that our love is unconditional, even when he tells us that he hates us.

A Tough Combination

Mixing ADHD and RAD together makes life very difficult for Wallace. He desperately wants to be *neurotypical* and not have these issues. Wallace cooperates with his counselors, psychiatrist, and other mental health providers, which is a huge step toward making progress. Mostly, Wallace has shown improvement over time. It is a huge challenge for Elisabeth and me, and we have had very difficult moments with Wallace, but we love our son unconditionally.

Name an Organ of the Body (above the Chest) That Begins with B

I wrote this book in part to show that life with a foreign adopted child can be a wonderful life-changing event for child and parents. Wallace, Elisabeth, and I have so much joy in our lives. It may sound goofy, but we sometimes cry at violin concerts, basketball games, and whenever Wallace has a good day at school.

It would be misleading, however, to say that we never have bad days in the Rankin house. Elisabeth and I have made mistakes as parents, and Wallace can have very challenging behaviors. We have lost friends and become estranged from family members because of issues with our parenting or Wallace's behaviors. As much as we love Wallace, love itself is not the complete answer for Wallace. Mental healthcare providers are a large part of our lives.

With no other subtle way to transition, I must take a moment to discuss appendicitis. (Now *that* is a left turn.) If your coworker has an appendectomy and misses a few days of work, you probably do not think any less of the person. If a family member, God forbid, gets cancer and goes through chemotherapy (and lives), you would find no stigma attached to the person.

Likewise, if a person has a traumatic brain injury and survives, that person most likely returns to "normal" life without any stigma. Therefore, a child with abnormal brain development should be able to receive treatment without feeling like they have a bad secret. The problem with abnormal brain development is that the symptoms are often behavioral in nature. Our society often views a person with behavioral issues as someone to shun—and certainly hospitalization should be kept a secret.

I believe that people with mental health diagnoses should have the ability to openly discuss their medical conditions in the same way a person with a disease of another organ of the body can discuss theirs. For this reason, I did not shy away from discussing Wallace's, and our whole family's, struggles with ADHD and RAD.

With Thanks

Well, here we are at the end of the book. This is known as *backmatter* in the publishing world.[52] Thank you for reading my book. I have started a sequel, but that will take some time.

Feel free to stop by www.tomtheauthor.com for updates and untraditional SPAM recipes.

---

52 Many people think this is a sly reference to the 1980s British sitcom, *Blackadder*. In that vein, let me state, Additional Dialogue by William Shakespeare.

About the Author

Tom is an attorney in Jamestown, New York. Prior to becoming an attorney, Tom worked in higher education administration and also taught English in Japan for almost three years. In his spare time, Tom likes to launch model rockets, collect stamps, yodel, and test Elisabeth's patience. Tom was also recently voted the second most handsome attorney in Jamestown.

Contributor

I thank all of the people who made this book possible. I especially thank Robert Macullar for his generosity

~